What people a

Concepts for a Democrat

In his past writings, the Bulgarian social activist and political researcher Yavor Tarinski has demonstrated a singular talent for explaining concepts in political and social theory in an engaging and highly accessible manner. Now he has put forward a compelling manifesto for radically transforming society toward a non-statist model of ecological direct democracy. This work draws substantially upon Tarinski's two main influences, the social theorists and critics Cornelius Castoriadis and Murray Bookchin, and also synthesizes ideas from such well-known thinkers as Hannah Arendt, David Graeber, Elinor Ostrom, David Harvey, and a host of other European and international sources.

Tarinski's text examines the fundamental conflict between democratic aspirations and the imposed norms of capitalism, the potential for directly democratic and ecologically designed cities, the imperative to renew the commons, and the prospects for a genuine solidarity economy to overturn the ravages of capitalist economic growth. He critiques bureaucratic, technocratic, and conspiracist tendencies both in mainstream discourse and on the Left, and offers a compelling and uplifting vision of a thoroughly transformed social order. This book is an important contribution to the expanding international literature in social ecology and democratic theory, and deserves to be read and discussed widely.

Brian Tokar, author of *Towards Climate Justice*

Yavor Tarinski's book gives us a good thrill of citizen empowerment and grassroots resistance. It presents direct democracy as a modern project for a new politics of equality

and solidarity. Just what we need today.
Vincent Gerber, author of *Bookchin and Social Ecology: An Intellectual's Biography*

Yavor Tarinski's *Concepts for a Democratic and Ecological Society* challenges your mind on the most significant questions such as direct democracy, de-growth, solidarity economy, and libertarian municipalism. This is a necessary revolutionary work which should be in your library to make you think more in depth about your future, about utopias, and ultimately about the perspectives of a democratic and ecological society.
Emet Değirmenci, author of *Women's Activism in Ecological Transformation*

Never has the vital vocabulary of socioeconomic integration and participation been more important. Yavor Tarinski has delivered us from forms of corporate cognitive conscription. Now, superfluous labels fall away. Let us take up appropriate direct action in the historical context of liberation struggles. Authenticity and autonomy arise.
Mark Mason, international commentator

The last work of Yavor Tarinski, *Concepts for a Democratic and Ecological Society*, is a great and holistic contribution to the change we urgently need to make in face of the Anthropocene era rooted in statecraft, capitalism, and authoritarianism. Based on the exploration of emancipatory movements of the last decades, from the alter-globalist struggles to recent local practices of resistance and mutual aid from all over the world, Yavor shares through his deep and simple words the meaningful path of social ecology. An invitation to free ourselves in all the fields of life, from democracy and education to the economic relations of domination. Through his accurate analysis of the current global situation based on many references to important intellectual figures like Bookchin, Castoriadis, Henri Lefebvre, etc, he invites us to begin to believe in the "magnificent life, waiting just around the corner" and create it, here and now.

Magali Fricaudet, member of *Institut d'écologie sociale et de communalisme.*

Concepts for a Democratic and Ecological Society

Concepts for a Democratic and Ecological Society

Yavor Tarinski

Winchester, UK
Washington, USA

JOHN HUNT PUBLISHING

First published by Zero Books, 2022
Zero Books is an imprint of John Hunt Publishing Ltd., No. 3 East St., Alresford,
Hampshire SO24 9EE, UK
office@jhpbooks.com
www.johnhuntpublishing.com
www.zero-books.net

For distributor details and how to order please visit the 'Ordering' section on our website.

ISBN: 978 1 78904 922 0
978 1 78904 923 7 (ebook)
Library of Congress Control Number: 2021935027

A CIP catalogue record for this book is available from the British Library.

Design: Stuart Davies

UK: Printed and bound by CPI Group (UK) Ltd, Croydon, CR0 4YY
Printed in North America by CPI GPS partners

We operate a distinctive and ethical publishing philosophy in
all areas of our business, from our global network of authors to
production and worldwide distribution.

Contents

Preface

Yavor Tarinski's *Concepts for a Democratic and Ecological Society* challenges your mind on the most significant questions such as direct democracy, de-growth, solidarity economy, and libertarian municipalism.

Yavor Tarinski positions democracy against hierarchies that span from gerontocracy to patriarchal perspectives. Then, he links this concept to the anti-globalization movement from Seattle in 1999, through the World Social Forum of Porto Alegre, the Occupy Wall Street in New York, the Indignados of Madrid and Barcelona, the Nuit Debout in Paris in the following years, and the more recent Yellow Vests of France.

Tarinski analyses the rebel city movement in the context of municipalism and direct democracy experiences. He takes us on a journey starting from the ancient Athenian polis which is considered to be the birthplace of democracy but was not inclusive of slaves, women, and the poor. We are then shown how democracy has evolved in Italian cities in the Middle Ages between the ninth and fifteenth centuries, and how the French Commune in 1871 contributed to the principles of democratic politics – a significant event during which Paris became a public space through neighborhood assemblies.

Although Tarinski tries to balance his research with a reference section from a gender perspective, the revolutionary French women's struggle is not included. Their obvious demand is ignored in history. For instance, on October 5, 1789 the Women's March on Versailles was not only for requisition of bread's fair price. A social history study underlines that the:

> ...march to Versailles was an extension of the long-accepted role of ordinary women in eighteenth-century Paris. The nature of women's paid and unpaid work, of female religious

1

observance, and of the individual and collective identity that these created, gave women a key role in defending the local community. This led them to act politically well before the Revolution. Their action in October 1789 was consistent with patterns of behavior shaped by everyday life in the city. Yet the scale of the action and its city-wide character were quite unlike anything that had happened before. In this, the lesson of July 1789 was important, but so were long-term changes in Paris. The city was becoming more integrated, both economically and administratively, and this gave working women a new relationship to urban space.[1]

Direct democracy is especially analyzed in depth. For example, it is emphasized that the Agora meetings within the public space discussed ideas and exchanged skills in a similar manner to an example from the near past – the Occupy movement, which began in New York in 2012 and spread all over the world. It came to show for yet another time that, unlike statecraft that is predisposed to bureaucratic centralization and hierarchy, cities tend to empower local populaces, creating citizens actively involved in public affairs.

Disadvantaged and marginalized groups of people such as the LGBTQIA + BIPOC, migrant and refugee communities, and many others that are being oppressed, become visible when their voices are heard during direct democracy practices. Social ecologists view the local level of neighborhood assemblies as the basis of the organizational model of democratic confederalism and it is logically interlinked with the strategy of libertarian municipalism. A version of it is currently being built in the Middle East in Rojava, northern Syria, and as the Zapatista movement in southern Mexico.

In regards to urbanization without ecological principles, most mega-cities today are urban sprawls. The megacity is a real problem because of their continuous economic growth.

The private, gated communities of these urban sprawls and their so-called smart cities paradigm leave no space for human connection. On the other hand, migrants and refugees are faced with an increasing urban militarization across the globe: as we saw in the city of Portland, USA, prior to the election of Trump, during the Gezi movement in Istanbul, Turkey, and in Barcelona, Spain as well.

On the topic of *Commons as Paradigm Beyond State and Markets*, Tarinski includes Elinor Ostrom's work from 1988, which responds to the *Tragedy of the Commons*. Ostrom discovered how local communities share irrigation, fisheries, and farmlands equally in the US, Guatemala, Turkey, Nepal, India, and elsewhere. However, exhaustion of commons is a possibility when there is no continuous community dynamic.

The narrative of constant economic growth, another topic analyzed by Tarinski, is based on a continuously-growing consumerist society. It results in an economism of which determinism is one of the main pillars. Economic determinism is based on the idea that it can be predicted what direction humanity will take in the future. It presents the economy as the most complex non-understandable organizational structure in a capitalist society and under state socialism, while it's structured in a quite hierarchical manner.

Whereas the solidarity economy, Tarinski argues, is an alternative that breaks with this deterministic logic, it allows people to express and meet their needs through creativity, by building from today new forms of production, consumption, and social relationships based on fundamentally different core principles such as direct democracy, trust, solidarity, and dignity. Much like the practices introduced by the Zapatistas and Rojava's Kurdish democratic communities, solidarity economies became a vision, especially after the 2008 economic crises. In this realm one encounters workers and consumer cooperatives, time banks, social currencies, and housing co-ops. Activist

Cheyenna Weber, co-founder of SolidarityNYC, describes such cooperative practices by suggesting that: "we focus on racial and social justice and by stewarding the commons we are encouraging people to move money from corporate investment to justice such as community land trust, farmland, etc."[2]

In his examination of what a just ecological society might look like, Tarinski not only criticizes the consumerist capitalist system, but also underlines the inconsistencies and problematics of authoritarian state socialism, which is missing from most political texts. In short, this is a necessary revolutionary work which should be in your library to make you think more in depth about your future, about utopias, and ultimately about the perspectives of a democratic and ecological society.

Introduction

When it is genuine, when it is born of the need to speak, no one can stop the human voice. When denied a mouth, it speaks with the hands or the eyes, or the pores, or anything at all. Because every single one of us has something to say to the others, something that deserves to be celebrated or forgiven by others.
Eduardo Galeano[3]

Nowadays we are witnessing a clash of significations. On the one side we have the forces of statecraft, capitalism, and authoritarianism that advance an oligarchic structure of society. Old concepts such as gerontocracy, patriarchy, and hierarchy are being rebranded and pushed on the majority of people as a natural part of the human condition.

On the other side, however, there is a vibrant grassroots activity that stems from our societies, which strives at emancipating them and allowing them to radically alter their political architecture. From the alter-globalist movement that began in Seattle in 1999, through the World Social Forum of Porto Alegre, Occupy Wall Street in New York, the Indignados of Madrid and Barcelona, the Nuit Debout in Paris, the Yellow Vests from all French towns and cities, social movements have challenged the dominant significations of our current social order and advanced different concepts that express the project of social and individual autonomy. Even under the harsh conditions of a global pandemic, with whole societies placed under lockdown, communities offered mutual aid to their most vulnerable members while states cared mainly for expanding the interests of the business class and their own political class as actions for holding onto power.

This book is an anthologizing of the recurring concepts charged with highly emancipatory and revolutionary potential that have sprung amid social movements and agonistic communities from different parts of the world. As we continue witnessing the innate inability of bureaucratic and capitalist mechanisms to look out for the common good, there is an increasingly existential need to seek other forms of social organizing that will give all members of society an equal share of control over their collective life.

Direct Democracy versus Capitalism

The most effective way to restrict democracy is to transfer decision-making from the public arena to unaccountable institutions: kings and princes, priestly castes, military juntas, party dictatorships, or modern corporations.
Noam Chomsky[4]

Nowadays the terms democracy and capitalism have often been used almost as synonyms. This interchangeability has penetrated not only the official political vocabulary but also social imaginaries. Many who feel oppressed and/or exploited by the current system tend to blame both concepts.

A significant faction of the Left also participates in this terminological equalization because it wrongly interprets democracy simply as a process dedicated to the guaranteeing of rights and liberties. But even so, philosopher Cornelius Castoriadis suggests that those who believe this are wrong because the emergence of rights and liberties was not an occurrence in the interests of capitalism.[5] According to him, these rights and liberties were demanded at the outset by the struggles of the underprivileged as well as by the inhabitants of the newly emerged free towns. Furthermore, he notes that these rights and liberties do not correspond to the spirit of capitalism: the latter demands, rather, the Taylorist "one best way" or the "iron cage" of Max Weber. The idea that they might be the political counterpart of and presupposition for competition in the economic market is equally false. When we consider the inner tendency of capitalism, Castoriadis continues, we see that capitalism culminates in monopoly, oligopoly, or alliances among capitalists.

The truth is that democracy, in its authentic direct form, has nothing to do with capitalism and is in fact at odds with it.

James Madison, one of the USA's Founding Fathers, seems to have been aware of this when claiming that democracies have ever been found incompatible with personal security or the rights of property.[6]

Capitalism as an engine of inequality

Democracy is a system of radical political equality. Hannah Arendt defines it as a political system that guarantees civil and political rights while allowing all willing citizens direct participation in government.[7] It places politics in charge of all spheres of social life. It is clear that this is not the system we have today.

Capitalism, on the other hand, nurtures social antagonisms that lead to social inequalities, and its proponents often openly defend inequality as a natural aspect of human nature.[8] In doing so, it places economics as a separate and supreme field of human interaction.

In a capitalist setting, people are pitted against each other to compete for resources, space, and time. It is not only economic classes competing with each other, but also people from similar social milieux. And where there is antagonism there always are winners and losers. Steven W. Thrasher concludes that "the disparities in wealth that we term 'income inequality' are no accident, they happened by design, and the system structurally disadvantages those at the bottom."[9] Furthermore, researchers D. B. Krupp and Thomas R. Cook suggest in a study that social inequalities are being amplified by local competition,[10] which is the cornerstone of free-market economics.

Anthropologist Jason Hickel exemplifies the way economic inequalities create and strengthen power discrepancies in the following way:

Every additional dollar that goes to the rich adds more to their power, and the richer they are, the more power it adds.

Why? Because the more distant the new money is from any given need threshold, the more it is available to be spent on power. The relationship between income and power is, in effect, an inverse logarithmic relationship. Plus, we need to account for the fact that the more money the rich spend on power, the more they inflate its price, pushing power ever-further out of the reach of the poor.[11]

Furthermore, although capitalism has often been presented as a non-bureaucratic system, in reality, it functions in a strictly hierarchical top-down manner. Iranian sociologist Jacob Rigi explains that:

labour is still compartmentalized in closed spaces and is managed despotically by representatives of capital. While a small select group of workers may enjoy partial autonomy the total labor process is centralized by managers who integrate the work of separate workers into a total cooperative work process…Individual producers do not choose their tasks, or the pace, time and place of their work. In other words the work process is micro-territorialized both spatially and temporally.[12]

In fact, bureaucracy was strengthened by the rise of capitalism. The latter was actually very dependent on bureaucratized structures and it thus nurtured them. Anthropologist David Graeber discovered in his research on the *Utopia of Rules* that market reforms always increase the total number of bureaucrats, as was the case with the Reagan administration, for example.[13] Social ecologist Murray Bookchin points to another historic example of this trend by claiming that "we in the United States 200 years ago started out with the notion of limited government — virtually no government interference — and we now have a massive quasi-totalitarian government."[14]

Democracy as a project of equality

As noted above, direct democracy (as the only real form of democracy) follows a completely different logic from capitalism. It is a political project that strives at radically redistributing decision-making power equally among all members of society. In doing so, it directly attacks all other forms of inequality as citizens undertake directly the management of all social spheres via public grassroots institutions. Instead of competition, it implies cooperation and equal participation.

Noam Chomsky underlines this stark difference:

Democracy...means that the central institutions in the society have to be under popular control. Now, under capitalism we can't have democracy by definition. Capitalism is a system in which the central institutions of society are in principle under autocratic control. Thus, a corporation or an industry is, if we were to think of it in political terms, fascist; that is, it has tight control at the top and strict obedience has to be established at every level – there's a little bargaining, a little give and take, but the line of authority is perfectly straightforward. Just as I'm opposed to political fascism, I'm opposed to economic fascism. I think that until major institutions of society are under the popular control of participants and communities, it's pointless to talk about democracy.[15]

By placing all power equally in the hands of all people, direct democracy abolishes the separation of the different spheres of social life. Judiciary, legislative, economic, cultural, and other issues are all discussed and decided upon in the public sphere by the empowered citizenry. It is the people collectively deciding the rules, norms, and limits of all their social activities, and they can alter them whenever the majority deems it necessary.

In this line of thought, then, Bookchin suggests that

democracy "politicizes the economy and dissolves it into the civic domain"[16]. In the democratic project, according to Bookchin, "'property' is integrated into the commune as a material constituent of its libertarian institutional framework, indeed as a part of a larger whole that is controlled by the citizen body in assembly as 'citizens,' not as vocationally oriented interest groups."[17]

Unlike economistic notions such as "nationalization" and "privatization," both implying the separation of the economy from politics, direct democracy advances the subjugation of economic activities along with all other social spheres to the political institutions of self-management. According to Bookchin, the economy ceases to be merely an economy in the strict sense of the word whether as "'business,' 'market,' 'capitalist', or 'worker-controlled' enterprises" and instead the citizen body in face-to-face assembly absorbs the economy as an aspect of the public sphere.[18] From this it follows that in the project of direct democracy, it will be more appropriate to speak of "municipalization" of the economy.

Conclusion

We have to understand that democracy, in its true meaning, is something much more than a mere procedure that can be used within other social systems. Conducting referendums on occasions, while maintaining the separation of power from society via state bureaucracies and/or capitalist markets, does not make one regime more democratic. It may give it a more humane face, but it remains an oligarchy nonetheless: a society ruled by a small minority.

As long as there are centralized and bureaucratic entities, regardless of their ideological mantle, we cannot talk of democracy. It is only when the people – as demos – self-empower themselves and begin self-instituting their collective coexistence that we can begin sowing the seeds of a democratic society.

As Castoriadis suggests:

rotation in office, sortition, decision-making after deliberation by the entire body politic, elections, and popular courts did not rest solely on a postulate that everyone has an equal capacity to assume public responsibilities: these procedures were themselves pieces of a political educational process, of an active paideia, which aimed at exercising – and, therefore, at developing in all – the corresponding abilities and, thereby, at rendering the postulate of political equality as close to the effective reality of that society as possible.[19]

Only by conceiving of democracy as a holistic project can we understand that it is not only incompatible with capitalist relations and statecraft, but it requires their complete abolition. As Prof Dr Wolfgang Merkel concludes: "capitalism and democracy follow different logics: unequally distributed property rights on the one hand, equal civic and political rights on the other; profit-oriented trade within capitalism in contrast to the search for the common good within democracy; debate, compromise and majority decision-making within democratic politics versus hierarchical decision-making by managers and capital owners."[20]

It is up to all of us collectively to make the choice of the twenty-first century – democracy or barbarism.

Rebel Cities and Libertarian Municipalism

With the rise of cities, a major power shift is occurring this century across the planet in both economic and political terms.
Dimitrios Roussopoulos[21]

Nowadays the importance of the city is increasing, not only because of the fact that the majority of the human population is currently living in urban areas, but also because of the global trend of cities exercising growing influence over national and transnational political, economic, social, environmental, and other affairs.[22] While the signing of the Westphalia Treaty in 1648 signified a period driven by the interests of nation-states, today we are entering into a new form dominated by transnational institutions, multinational corporations, and mega-cities.

In the contemporary capitalist system based on unlimited economic growth, the city's role is rapidly growing as it undoubtedly is becoming the world's GDP champion. This is increasingly evident from the fact that a few hundred cities across the planet account for more than half of the global GDP.[23] In economic terms these sub-national entities can thus be regarded less as a territory but as a space where global flows – capital, information, people, goods, services – crisscross and solidify. Antonio Negri has noted this economization of the urban space, suggesting that cities have become a source of production, just as worked land once was.[24] The city is increasingly becoming the central cog in the global economic machine.

The current trend in rapid urbanization has begun transforming the face of international affairs as well. Cities and local governments are increasingly undertaking mediatory roles in global relations due to their growing political and economic influence. The creation of transnational coordination bodies such as the Global Parliament of Mayors[25] and the Compact of Mayors[26] are indicative of the differentiation between the agendas followed by national and sub-national authorities. Cities are even formally joining multilateral institutions initially projected for nation-states like the World Trade Organization, the United Nations, and the World Tourism Organization. As with the city-states of the past, the contemporary urban entities are becoming increasingly independent polities in international affairs.

The military sphere of raw power is another field in which a shift of positions between the city and the state could be observed.[27] Contemporary researchers, thinkers, and activists, from disciplines ranging from urban geography to political science, tend to agree on the increasing role urban areas have in armed conflicts. The asymmetric powers of conflicting sides have increasingly led military strategists to take the battlefield to the complex and unpredictable terrain of contemporary mega-cities. Other factors such as refugee waves – caused variously by war, poverty, or climate change – additionally influence this trend. Thus, the monopoly of nation-states on military power is being contested by the growing militarization of cities across the globe. This new military urbanism has blurred, as the works of contemporary authors such as Mike Davis and Stephen Graham are demonstrating, the lines between armed combatants and civilian citizens. These conditions often result in the brutal crushing of the voices of active citizen dissent and instead reinforce further passive consumerist attitudes.

The current age of urbanization also presents certain challenges before humanity's health, as well as its footprint on the environment.[28] Urban sprawl that requires long commutes by car and little-to-no physical exercise, air and noise pollution, and other factors have resulted in new kinds of diseases and health problems that are affecting urban dwellers. But contemporary mega-cities are also representing potential and real threats to the environment with much more than half of both the global energy consumption and greenhouse gas emissions resulting from ongoing urbanization. Cities consume enormous amounts of resources as well as threaten water supplies with pollution. In short, the future of the natural environment on this planet is directly linked with the future of the cities in which most of us currently live.

From the statements above we can understand the growing importance of the city in modern life. Notions such as "cultural capital" and "creative cities" indicate the role urban spaces are undertaking in spheres beyond the ones we have taken for granted. From here we can agree with Negri that the inhabitant of a metropolis has become the true center of the world[29] since the future of the city, and of humanity, is in the hands of the citizen and their fellow citizens.

The city as public space

[M]any city centers became dominated by leisure use. It was of course a commercial rather than an anarchic leisure, since larger situationist demands remained marginalized by capitalism – which always seemed likely to be the case, except perhaps for a few heady days in May 1968.
Simon Sadler[30]

For thinkers such as Cornelius Castoriadis and Murray Bookchin, the historic emergence of the city is interlinked with the birth of democracy. It produced the notion of citizenry; that is, a community bonded not by clan or blood-ties but by political agreement. This urban politics allowed for the creation of public spaces that enabled citizens to collectively manage their cities which laid the foundations of direct democracy. Not all cities were democratic. In fact, most were managed in an oligarchic manner but their foundational logic has strengthened the concept of participatory politics.

The period of antiquity saw the emergence of the ancient Athenian polis and the birth of democracy. They both were rooted in the idea of radical political equality among all citizens. This deeply democratic notion allowed the citizenry (up to 30,000 citizens at times) to conceive of history as creation and build the polis around such participatory institutions as the general assembly (ekklesia) and council of delegates (boule), in which magistrates were chosen by lot (sortition). These processes of self-instituting and the imaginary they simultaneously were embodying and nurturing allowed popular creativity to develop to levels unseen until today.

Then, in the Middle Ages (between the ninth and fifteenth centuries), many Italian cities became sites of wide popular liberation. People found refuge in them and the public space they created allowed them to throw off the authority of prince, king, or emperor. In their place a system of governance was introduced through interlocking and balanced councils. Large deliberative assemblies, comprising one hundred, two hundred, or more adult males, elected or chosen by lot, debated and created laws. Executive committees, often consisting of six, eight, or a dozen men, elected for 2-to-6 months, put the laws into action. Short terms in office and rules against self-succession made it possible for several hundred or more adult males to participate in government in a few years. The system of balanced and diffused power ensured that no individual or family could control the city. It was a government of balanced power and mutual suspicion.

In France, one of the most significant examples of the right to the city took place in the form of the Paris Commune of 1871. Although this urban popular uprising was crushed on May 27, 1871 by the French state's army, for a couple of months the city of Paris became real public space, managed directly by its citizens. The Paris communards, through neighborhood assemblies, took care of the important local administration.

These assemblies appointed revocable delegates to participate in councils, forming confederations through which they effectively coordinated production and redistribution.

A century later, in 1980, in the South Korean city of Gwangju, the people rose up in the so-called Gwangju people's revolt. The preconditions for it were an authoritarian government and the widespread poverty of this period, whereas the proximate cause was the brutality of paramilitary groups toward protesters. The people of Gwangju revolted, driving the military forces out of the city. The revolt lasted only 3 weeks but during this short period neighborhood assemblies emerged, giving voice to the local populace. Connecting with one another, these basic institutions of direct democracy maintained order and organized distribution in the city. The revolt was crushed by government forces on May 27 – the same date as the fall of the Paris Commune.

In all these and many other cases, such as Barcelona from 1936-39, Budapest in 1956, and Shanghai in 1967, cities became truly public spaces that emancipated the local populations into active citizenries. In their short lifespans, these radical urban experiences offered practical examples of new ways of everyday life and of democratic politics in general that can be employed today by social movements, not as ready blueprints to be blindly followed, but as germs that can spark the democratic and ecological transformation of our urban environment.

However, a big obstacle for people today in taking back their cities is the contemporary societal imaginary, viewing, as Richard Sennett suggests, the public space as "meaningless."[31] Sennett points at the nineteenth century, a period of rapid urbanization and economic growth, during which the outcome of the crisis of public culture, despite several urban eruptions of radical citizen activity, was that people lost a sense of themselves as an active force, as a public[32]. Sennett suggests that during this period an important role in the process of depriving the public space of meaning was the adoption of more uniform dress and behavior codes, more passive demeanor, and less sociability, all of which can be seen as byproducts of the emerging consumerist culture and logic of representation of that period. As Peter G. Goheen says: "The street became the place for illusion rather than exposure to the truth."[33] In a sense, the public man was supplanted by the spectator who did not so much participate in the public life of the city as observe it.

In order to overcome this point of view we are in need of new significations, which give back meaning to the public space. These can emerge only through practices of collectivities of citizens (the public) that would have positive and practical effects on the everyday life of society. Such processes are already taking place in the countryside and the villages. Because of the crisis, many people in countries such as Greece and Spain are leaving city life behind, returning to the villages that their parents and grandparents once fled.[34] In the countryside, city youth rediscover communal ways of life, the sharing of common resources, and recover traditional and ecological agricultural practices. But for the majority of those who undertake such steps, the village is an escape route from the uncertainty of the city, a form of escapism rather than part of a political project for social change. It neglects the role cities play in our societies and the potential they contain for the creation of one democratic and ecological future.

As for those who remain in the cities living under conditions of growing precarity, unemployment, and stress, the future does not seem so bright with harsh austerity measures still on the horizon. Discontent is producing uprisings and mass mobilizations in urban areas, ranging from Istanbul's Gezi Park, Ferguson's uprisings against police brutality, the anti-World Cup riots in Brazilian cities, and the Occupy and Indignados movements in the squares of major cities around the world. In all of these cases, in one way or another, the question of urban planning is being posed: can the city square obtain the role of the main cell of public deliberation, that is, simultaneously *agora* (meeting and exchange point) and basic decision-making body. Should a global festival of consumerism, such as the World Cup, have the right to reshape the urban landscape, regardless of human suffering; and who should decide if an urban green space (such as Gezi Park) is to be covered with concrete and transformed completely?

Potential solutions to this loss of meaning should be sought in projects of direct democracy that can once again make the city a truly public space. Or as Henri Lefebvre suggests, to take "the urban" beyond mere urbanization and toward a non-capitalist society characterized by meaningful engagement among inhabitants embedded in a web of social connections.[35]

Libertarian municipalism

Our teloi, which include a rationally and democratically constituted system of laws – of duties as well as rights – include as well this ability to be citizens, that is to say, to be educated in order to be competent to assume all the obligations of self-government.
Murray Bookchin[36]

Concepts such as libertarian municipalism, which are essentially direct-democratic, could be of great use in our efforts to regain our right to the city. Such notions are rooted in the historic clash over power between the municipality and the nation-state. Unlike statecraft, predisposed to bureaucratic centralization and hierarchy, cities tend to empower local populaces, creating citizens actively involved in public affairs. Today, however, with cities being submitted to the dominant imaginary significations, they are abandoning their previous role of socializing public space and becoming instead sprawling urban monsters, absorbing traditional cultures and producing alienation: new strategies are needed. Libertarian municipalism is among these strategies for reinvention of the city.

It is a political concept, developed initially by libertarian theorists such as Murray Bookchin and Janet Biehl, but has since been highly influential among radical political tendencies and has encouraged the practical creation of direct-democratic decision-making bodies, as popular assemblies and councils, in urban neighborhoods and towns. It seeks to potentially create suitable conditions for citizens to be able to take back control of their cities.

A distinctive feature of libertarian municipalism is its transcendence beyond narrow class analysis as advocated by some traditional ideological trends among Marxists and classical anarchists.[37] While not neglecting the worker exploitation occurring at the capitalist workplace, it asks us to challenge all forms of domination within society; that is, it strives at eliminating the dominance over workers as well as over women, ethnic minorities, young and old, handicapped, LGBT people, and whoever else is being oppressed.

Libertarian municipalism encourages dual power in which the authority of the state is being challenged by the self-empowered local democratic municipalities.[38] And while relatively peaceful coexistence could be expected initially, logically a conflict between the two is expected to emerge sooner or later. Thus emerges the need for collaboration between such liberated cities.

In this line of thought, libertarian municipalism does not necessarily seek momentary and violent revolution. Instead, it focuses on the educational qualities of the creation and spread of truly public space and time through the construction of a direct-democratic citizenry from bottom-to-top. Libertarian municipalism views the practical installation of such participatory institutions as the neighborhood assembly and the municipal council as potential educational tools for the nurturing of popular culture of active citizenship.

Historically speaking, independent municipalities tend to join forces into confederal alliances, not only for protection from common enemies, but also for sharing resources and knowledge. Social ecologists call this organizational model democratic confederalism and it is logically interlinked with the strategy of libertarian municipalism. Its target is to lay the foundations of one truly emancipated society. Instead of a centralized state apparatus governing the populace, it proposes the direct democracy of local decision-making bodies for self-management, networking with one another through regional confederations, thus rendering the state obsolete.

A version of it is currently being built in the Middle East by the communities of Rojava (northern Syria). There the Kurdish liberation movement, after a radical change in its political orientation, began establishing local, but interlinked, participatory decision-making bodies, independent from the official Syrian state authorities. This strategy demonstrated its strength in the period that followed the Arab Spring, when after the Syrian regime lost its control of the area, a new confederacy of democratic structures managed to get the local populations back on their feet, improve their living conditions, and defend them from the armed Jihadist gangs that terrorized the region.

The synthesis between libertarian municipalism and democratic confederalism aims toward a permanent social revolution. It aims to radicalize and emancipate one city after another through local municipal platforms and then connect these rebel cities through confederal coordinated bodies. In this way the current functions of state and private/capitalist entities will be undertaken by the emancipated demos.

Recently, with the rise of various municipal electoral platforms across Europe and abroad, there has been a certain trend in overlapping libertarian municipalism with citizen involvement in local elections. But although the initial developers of the project gave municipal electoralism a certain role within it, they in no way saw it as the main tool of social change. Instead, Bookchin and his followers sought in local elections nothing but another tool for the advancement of the ideas of direct democracy.[39] The municipal level, they thought, was not as centralized as the national one, and thus much more vulnerable to pressure and control by social movements.

Emancipatory urban design

The city is not merely a repository of pleasures. It is the stage on which we fight our battles, where we act out the drama of our own lives. It can enhance or corrode our ability to cope with everyday challenges. It can steal our autonomy or give us the freedom to thrive.
Charles Montgomery[40]

The oppressive status quo reproduces itself on many fronts. The pseudo-representative politics at the heart of it are designed to maintain the same patterns of thinking, no matter what the final electoral result is. The same goes for bureaucratic capitalist economic relations. The very cities where most of humanity lives are designed according to the dominant capitalist values and perceptions. They are dispersed, their inhabitants live in isolated private condominiums, distanced away from schools and workplaces and market districts, getting around alone in their private cars. This model of urban sprawl is rapidly spreading all over the world.[41] The cities are organized in such ways that human contact is greatly reduced. Thus, achieving social change in a more participatory and collaborative direction would be an overwhelmingly difficult task if we don't have this in our mind.

For society to be reorganized on the basis of direct democracy, the many preconditions that seem to be required include the breaking of alienation and the establishment of communitarian relationships. A city that would encourage and strengthen community feeling would represent a mixture of housing, public areas, schools, workplaces, shopping, green, and other spaces, all of which would be within walking distance or reachable by public transportation, in contrast with the modern capitalist way of urban land use, based on the positioning of fixed, single-use zones across vast distances.

A mixed land use consisting of medium-sized housing cooperatives, with adjoined gardens, within a walking distance from schools, public squares, markets, and green spaces would allow for the experience of random interactions between neighbors. The walking element could build a feeling of belonging into the city, with citizens developing strong links with their local, social, and urban environment. It would also, as author Jay Walljasper notes,[42] contribute to greater economic equality by allowing everyone the right to freely move across the city, without the need for a car.

The shift toward walkable cities would imply the radical rethinking and remaking of roads and streets, today designed mainly as high-speed arteries connecting housing districts with office areas, encouraging driving over walking. As Donald Appleyard's famous 1972 study demonstrates,[43] the heavier the car traffic on a street is, the fewer are the walkers and the everyday communal experiences. This, in addition to the obvious effects on human health which lead to obesity, heart disease, and other conditions, contributes to the already high levels of alienation in urban areas.

An approach that could alter this alienating effect, encouraging people to instead walk on the streets and potentially produce community feeling, is the narrowing of streets in urban areas, the expansion of pedestrian spaces, and the introduction of wider bicycle alleys. As the city planner and author Jeff Speck explains,[44] people drive faster when they have less fear of veering off track, so wider lanes invite higher speeds. This, in mixture with a vast network of free urban public transportation, would allow for daily social interactions on them by pedestrians and passengers. The daily social experiences like noddings, smiles, and random chatting with co-citizens could potentially make us feel more comfortable on our streets.

This in turn would bring with it other positive effects as well, such as drastic reductions of the health problems mentioned earlier, but also a reduction of car speeds which are responsible for the deaths of huge numbers of people around the world, as well as reduction of the air pollution of the contemporary private car-dominated metropolises.

Green spaces are another key aspect of the urban environment. According to Bob Lalasz, they generally make people happier.[45] Furthermore, green spaces tend to bring people closer together if planned and designed in an appropriate manner.[46] Thus in a community-promoting urban project, nature should be an essential part of the urban landscape. The gardens, part of housing cooperatives, will allow for the experience of gardening time by neighbors, bonding them together. They will also potentially encourage the development of a communal/ solidarity economy by neighbors producing their own food and exchanging or sharing it with other urban gardeners.

In addition, parks and public gardens should be shuffled across the mixed urban land uses. Modern metropolitan cities trend toward approving large-scale parks too zoned away from housing districts and office areas, making human interaction with nature a rare opportunity. Contrary to that logic, the mixed-use city, as described here, could comprise green spaces located in various locations across the city. As Charles Montgomery suggests,[47] this does not exclude the existence of large-scale parks but the urban green space will not be limited to them. This will imply that people will have the opportunity to get in contact with tiny gardens and parks on their way to work for example, as well as to experience the feeling of going "into the wild" by entering the huge local parks.

Public squares play a key role in a city that encourages communitarian culture and citizenry, since they act as spaces for social interactions as well as forums for the expression of civic opinions. Thus they should be made freely available for popular interventions, unlike today, where bureaucrats decide who, when, and for what reason they should be used.

However, we also hear critiques about the overcrowding of modern cities leading to further alienation and withdrawal into passivity. If this is true, should we abandon city life altogether and return to village life? According to psychologist Andrew Baum's study,[48] the feeling of over-crowdedness is being fed by urban design that does not allow people to control the intensity of spontaneous social interactions. Baum compared the behavior of residents of two very different college dormitories. He concluded that students whose environment was allowing them to control their social interactions experienced less stress and built more friendships than students who lived within long and crowded corridors.

Therefore an answer to the problem of overcrowding could be found in the creation of semi-public/communal spaces, which represent a middle ground between the private and the public. This would imply the abandonment of the gigantic housing projects in which large numbers of people live together such as the socialist-era gigantic worker barracks, never feeling quite alone. Instead, a space could be given to medium-sized housing cooperatives with common spaces in disposal of all the neighbors. In this way, three layers of social spheres would be created: private, communal, and public. Such arrangements would allow citizens to regulate their social interaction, thus giving them a sense of comfort and encouraging egalitarianism.

Transcending of capitalism and the state

The right to the city is far more than the individual liberty to access urban resources: it is a right to change ourselves by changing the city.
David Harvey[49]

During the last few years the city has emerged as a potential contender to the nation-state in a global wave that can be characterized as a "rebellion of the municipal." The radical geographer David Harvey has even argued that "rebel cities" will become a preferred site for revolutionary movements.[50] This new rebellious municipalist trend bears heavily on the theoretical influence of the work of libertarian thinker Murray Bookchin who, like the philosopher Cornelius Castoriadis, returned to the forgotten ancient Athenian concept of the *Polis* as a credible source for solutions to the ills of our contemporary society. He attempted with great success to reveal the revolutionary essence of this notion and its potentialities for our times. To parliamentary oligarchy, tribal nationalism, and capitalist relations, Bookchin proposed direct-democratic confederations of libertarian municipalities where citizens participate directly in local assemblies and elect revocable delegates to regional councils. In the city and its historic rivalry with the state, he saw a possible public space where civic culture can break domination in all its forms.

This legacy seems, more than ever, abreast with our time. Although large cities worldwide are increasingly following their own agendas that often go against state policies, such as the city of London and its resistance to Britain's leaving of the EU (the so-called Brexit),[51] a new generation of municipal platforms is emerging boosted by the deepening of the crisis of representation. Most of them are partially influenced by the above-mentioned theoretical framework, and have sprung up in different parts of the world, but mainly in Europe. In Spain, such projects govern most major cities such as Barcelona and Madrid.[52] These platforms are trying to reverse the austerity measures that are being enforced by the state, international technocratic institutions and transnational agreements, re-municipalize basic public services, introduce participatory decision-making bodies at a local level, feminize politics, and challenge governmental anti-migrant policies. Some of these rebel cities have begun connecting with each other, thus multiplying and strengthening their voices.

In the USA as well, local municipalities have reached into conflict with the central government's policies. Close to 250 cities across the country have pledged to adopt, honor, and uphold the commitments to the goals set by the Paris Climate Agreements after the announcement of President Trump's plans to break up with the latter.[53] Although the motivations of some of these local administrations remain questionable due to their possible connections with the main electoral opponents to the contemporary government, municipal platforms are emerging in the USA as well, including the initiative *Olympia for All*[54] that tries to give more participatory and ecological characteristics to the municipality of Olympia, Washington (USA).

Of course, there are problems with these practices. Most of these municipal projects attempt to radicalize cities through the mechanisms of local bureaucracies that resemble to a large degree the state apparatus. This fact raises the question of how far this so-called radicalization can go. Why should the installation of militants from social movements in the hierarchical municipal administration succeed if it has failed to do so disastrously on the national level several times during the revolutionary experiences of the last 2 centuries?

We should consider the difficulty of balancing between city bureaucracy and social movements. It is well known that especially in Europe, these municipal platforms (most notably

Barcelona en Comu) emerged from the so-called movement of the squares that attempted redefining and reclaiming a more authentic notion of democracy. But if the essence of the real, direct democracy is the abolition of the bureaucratic fragmentation of everyday life, can it then be advanced with bureaucratic means such as political representation and expertism? In the end, as the old maxim goes, the means determine the goal and the direction. You cannot learn democracy if you do not practice it.

However, all these problems cannot make us abandon the city as a potential locus for making politics beyond statecraft, but instead provoke us to rethink it as truly public space that is constantly being recreated by its citizens and that goes beyond narrow electoralism. It raises questions of crucial importance like how local politicians can be turned into municipal delegates, that serve the neighborhood assemblies and are constantly revocable by those that have elected them. In more general terms, the question they pose is how the city's administration can be integrated into the democratic vision, forwarded in practice by "the squares." Answers to these and many more problematics will not come easy, but should be developed patiently in deliberative manner "from below" if we want to avoid this new municipalist revolt to drift away from its acclaimed democratic goals and descend into localized forms of representative oligarchy with a friendlier face.

One contemporary case that seems to be going in the right direction, although in a completely different socio-historical context from Euro-American culture, is the democratic autonomy that is currently being built in Rojava, northern Syria. The base of the confederal system that nowadays functions in this part of the war-torn Middle East was set through a strategy that resembles to a large degree the principles of libertarian municipalism, as noted earlier in this text. And while structures that resemble to a certain extent representative democracy coexist with participatory grassroots institutions there, militants from the TEV-DEM movement[55] together with activists from the local communities are constantly searching for ways to make sure that power in their society flows from the bottom to the top. Their success is quite impressive, managing to establish one of the most politically inclusive self-governance systems in the world.

The authoritarian nature of the contemporary dominant system requires anti-authoritarian alternative paradigms if it is to be successfully challenged. Although many have argued that the current rise in authoritarianism and technocracy is nothing but a temporary phase in the liberal oligarchic rule, others, such as Walter Benjamin, have argued that the "state of exception" in which we live is in fact not the exception but the rule. Electoral victories by far-right candidates and fascist parties are not some sort of systemic breakdown but the continuation of traditional hierarchical rule by other means. Thus it is up to all of us, of those below, to bring about a real exception in the tradition of heteronomy and follow a democratic tradition instead by radically breaking up with the domination of human-over-human and humanity over nature.

The way through which this could be achieved logically cannot circulate around the ballot box, either on the national or local level, but needs to be focused on the self-organization and self-institution of society itself. This would imply communities organizing independently from established bureaucracies and determining their agendas for themselves. Movements of urban commoners and libertarian municipalists should join forces, as their paradigms have the potential to transform our cities along democratic and ecological lines.

We already saw in the last decade that the popular resistances in urban areas have adopted an anti-authoritarian approach with democratic characteristics. Vanguardist structures like parties and syndicates, once dominant among social movements, have nowadays been abandoned and replaced by open participatory institutions. Demonstrations are increasingly turning into reclamation of public spaces and commons. Thus we can speak of general social attempts at redefining the right to the city.

The role of social movements in these processes would not be to lead, but to nurture these direct-democratic traits that stem from our very societies. Among the main questions for them should be how to manage to successfully locate and maintain the grassroots institutions that are emerging in public squares and city neighborhoods in the short eruptions of civil disagreement with enforced policies "from above." How their character could be transformed from purely symbolic to effective and decision-making institutions is a strategic question. This also puts forward the need for regional and even transnational connectedness between such dispersed local grassroots institutions for them to be able to function sustainably in the face of state and capitalist hostility. For such germs of genuine direct democracy we could also look beyond the contemporary Western world to cities such as Cochabamba (Bolivia)[56] and Porto Alegre (Brazil),[57] and in the radical urban tradition that goes as far as the ancient Athenian *Polis*.

Conclusion

A magnificent life is waiting just around the corner, and far, far away. It is waiting like the cake is waiting when there's butter, milk, flour and sugar. This is the realm of freedom.
Henri Lefebvre[58]

As Castoriadis has suggested, we are at a crossroads in the path of history.[59] Some of the more visible paths will keep us within heteronomy in worlds dominated by the barbarism of international agreements and technocratic institutions, state apparatuses, and nationalist cannibalism. Although the characteristics of each one of them may differ, their base remains essentially the same: elites and predetermined truths dominating society and nature. Humanity has been living within this framework during most of its recent history and the symptoms are painfully familiar to us all: loss of meaning, conformism, apathy, irresponsibility, the tightening grip of unlimited economic growth, pseudo-rational pseudo-mastery, consumption for the sake of consumption, and techno-science that strengthens the domination of capitalist imaginary.

There is, however, another road that is not brightly visible but always existent. Unlike the above-mentioned directions that are being determined by extra-social sources, this one has to be opened and laid through the political practice of all citizens and their will for freedom. This road requires the abolition of the bureaucratic fragmentation of everyday life which is the essence of the state, reclamation of the public space, the commons, and the *Polis*, reawakening the creative imaginary and the re-articulation of the project of autonomy. But it is a matter of social and individual political choice which road our societies will take and the main arena where the final choice will have to be taken will most probably be the city.

Political Ecology: Overcoming Technocracy and Capitalist "Needs"

For some decades now human civilization has embarked on a journey to rapidly extract whatever resources it can from the planet so as to maintain its current predominant doctrine — unlimited economic growth. There are, as one could imagine, dire consequences resulting from this activity that place our very future in danger. Despite the dangers that go together with the growth doctrine, we are being told to blindly direct our hopes toward science as the ultimate crisis resolver, to clean up the mess left from extreme extractivism.

Science and technology today have become the practical equivalent of religion. They have managed to reinforce the dominant ideological mystification in a time in which authority has become ostensibly desacralized. If in the past the power of the ruling elites was explained through its divine God-given origin, today it rests on the scientific knowledge that they claim to possess, and allows them to continue their destructive activities.

The emerging new totalitarian forms are being described as technocracies – rule by experts and technicians. The very structure of contemporary techno-science resembles the dominant organizational structure of society – that of heteronomy.

The depth this logic has reached is even more evident from the space it occupies among youth counter-cultures. If in the Sixties they were deeply submerged into radical politics from below, modern-day hacker culture, for example, has given birth to supposedly-alternative tendencies such as the Zeitgeist movement, in which technological and scientific expertise has replaced popular self-instituting governance, thus essentially reproducing the heteronomous nature of the present system.

Need, as social creation

As with religious sacralized regimes of the past, contemporary technocracies claim to know what the people actually need. They claim they can calculate it through the means of science and deliver it through economic growth and extraction. But what they actually do is to express the needs embedded in one specific imaginary. In reality we can say that there are no predetermined natural human needs. Every society creates its needs and the means for their satisfaction. For one truly religious person the ultimate need is to make a pilgrimage to a holy (to his faith) place, spending all his savings if required. For the anthropological type of capitalism, the need to constantly replace his belongings and gadgets with newer ones, that are slightly different and supposedly improved, seems as unquestionable and as natural as their very existence. Thus the term "need" is a social construct that can be altered.

If this paradigm today manages to function it does so because it successfully manages to provide the means for satisfaction of the needs it fabricates. And the debate between the two opposing fractions for the seats of power — the Right and the Left — is centered on this matter. The right-wingers advocate market deregulation as an engine of growth, while the leftist forces often tend to blame the current close ties between multinationals and governments on the lessened buying power of local populations and promise, if elected to power, to fix that. Both sides insist on the scientific nature of their claims. In this sense the current paradigm is less threatened by traditional ideological criticism than by fears of running out of oil, for example.

Ecology as a tool for the reinvention of politics

Bearing this in mind, contemporary ecological struggles and movements should detach themselves from narrow reformist environmentalism. Instead they should attempt to reconfigure the relations between humanity and nature, radically democratize society, and ultimately offer new imaginary significations so as to make another, more sustainable, way of life possible. Thus a political alternative will be offered to technocratic-excused social and environmental exploitation.

The rejection of the capitalist way of life, so as to have today any meaning beyond electoralism and green consumerism, should go hand-in-hand with the search for germs of other ways of life that contain traces of direct democracy, solidarity, self-limitation, and self-instituting or, in other words, seeds of autonomy; such germs that can satisfy certain contemporary needs but also reflect desires that are not being covered by the present social system.

Challenging the doctrine of constant capitalist growth requires serious rethinking of what our societies can do. The ecological movements constantly remind us of the fact that we all share the same planet. Thus the above-mentioned principles should be embedded in one framework that will allow society to constitute itself, while consciously self-limiting its affairs democratically inside the planetary boundaries. But this cannot be enforced from above, from an extra-social set of scientific knowledge or pseudo-enlightened elite. It can come only if society itself desires it, or it will not come at all. In its essence it is a political rather than scientific choice that our society has to make.

Analyzing the Commons beyond State and Capitalist Markets

People called commons those parts of the environment for which customary law exacted specific forms of community respect. People called commons that part of the environment which lay beyond their own thresholds and outside of their own possessions, to which, however, they had recognized claims of usage, not to produce commodities but to provide for the subsistence of their households.
Ivan Illich[60]

Introduction

In their book *The Economic Order & Religion (1945)* Frank H. Knight and Thomas H. Merriam argue that "social life in a large group with thoroughgoing ownership in common is impossible."[61] William F. Lloyd and later Garrett Hardin, in the same spirit, promoted the neo-Malthusian[62] term "tragedy of the commons,"[63] arguing that individuals acting independently and rationally according to their self-interest behave contrary to the best interests of the whole group by depleting some common-pool resource. Since then, the thesis that people are incapable of managing collectively, without control and supervision by institutions and authorities separated from society, has successfully infiltrated the social imaginary.

Even for big sections of the Left, resource management in common is viewed as utopian and therefore they prefer to leave it for the distant future, lingering instead between variations of private and statist forms of property.[64] Thus is maintained the dilemma of private-state management of common-pool resources which leads to the marginalization of other alternative forms.

But a great many voices, trying to break with this dipole,

were always present and are currently growing in numbers. For the autonomists Michael Hardt and Antonio Negri this is a false dilemma. According to them:

> The seemingly exclusive alternative between the private and the public corresponds to an equally pernicious political alternative between capitalism and socialism. It is often assumed that the only cure for the ills of capitalist society is public regulation and Keynesian and/or socialist economic management; and, conversely, socialist maladies are presumed to be treatable only by private property and capitalist control. Socialism and capitalism, however, even though they have at times been mingled together and at others occasioned bitter conflicts, are both regimes of property that excluded the common. The political project of instituting the common...cuts diagonally across these false alternatives.[65]

The falsity of the state-private dilemma can also be seen from the symbiotic-like relationship between the two supposed alternatives. Author and activist David Bollier points to the historic partnership between the two.[66] According to him, markets have benefited from the state's provisioning of infrastructure and oversight of investment and market activity, as well as its providing of free and discounted access to public forests, minerals, airwaves, research, and other public resources. On the other hand, the state depends upon markets as a vital source of tax revenue and jobs for people – and as a way to avoid dealing with inequalities of wealth and social opportunity, two politically explosive challenges.

At first sight it seems like we are left without any real option, because the two alternatives we are being told "from above" that are possible, are systemically leading to the same degree of enclosure that we saw earlier from which beneficiaries are tiny elites. But during recent times the paradigm of the commons has reemerged from the grassroots as a powerful and practical solution to the contemporary crisis and a step beyond the dominant dilemma. This alternative is emerging as a third way, since it goes beyond the state and the so-called free market and has been tested in practice by communities from the past and present.

The logic of the commons

The logic of the commons goes beyond the ontology of the nation-state and the "free" market. In a sense it presupposes that we live in a common world that can be shared by all of society without some bureaucratic or market mechanisms to enclose it. Thus, with no enclosure exercised by external managers competing with society and each other, the resources stop being scarce because there is no longer any interest in their quick depletion. Ivan Illich notes that "when people spoke about commons, iriai [Japanese forest commons], they designated an aspect of the environment that was limited, that was necessary for the community's survival, that was necessary for different groups in different ways, but which, in a strictly economic sense, was not perceived as scarce."[67] The logic of the commons is ever-evolving and rejects the bureaucratization of rights and essences, though it includes forms of communal self-control and individual self-limitation. Because of this it manages to synthesize the *social* with the *individual*.

The commons can be found all around the world in different forms: from indigenous communities resisting the cutting of rainforests, and Indian farmers fighting GMO crops, to open-source software, and movements for digital rights over the internet. The main characteristics that are found in each of them are the direct-democratic procedures of their management, the open design and manufacturing, accessibility, and constant involvement.

The commons have their roots deep in antiquity but through

constant renewal are exploding nowadays, adding to the indigenous communal agricultural practices new solidarity economic forms as well as high-tech FabLabs, alternative currencies, and many more. The absence of a strict ideological framework enhances this constant involvement.

The logic of the commons is deeply rooted in the experience of ancient Athens. The Greek-French philosopher Cornelius Castoriadis describes it as a period during which a free public space appeared.[68] Castoriadis depicts it as "a political domain which 'belongs to all'" (τα κοινα – the commons in Greek). The public ceased to be a private affair – that is, an affair of the king, the priests, the bureaucracy, the politicians, or/and the experts. Instead decisions on common affairs had to be made by the community.

The logic of the commons, according to the anthropologist Harry Walker,[69] could also be found in the communities of Peruvian-Amazonia, for whom the most desirable goods were not viewed as rival goods, in contrast with modern economics which assumes that if goods are enjoyed by one person they can't be enjoyed by another. The Peruvian-Amazonian culture was focused on sharing, on the enjoyment of what can be shared rather than privately consumed.

Swiss villages are a classic example of sustainable commoning. Light on this is shed by Elinor Ostrom and her field research into one of them.[70] In the Swiss village in question, local farmers tend private plots for crops but share a communal meadow for herd grazing. Ostrom discovered that in this case an eventual tragedy of the commons (hypothetical overgrazing) is prevented by villagers reaching to a common agreement that one is allowed to graze as much cattle as they can care for during the winter. And this practice dates back to 1517. Other practical and sustainable examples of effective communal management of commons Ostrom discovered are in the US, Guatemala, Kenya, Turkey, Nepal, and elsewhere.

Elinor Ostrom visited Nepal in 1988 to research the many farmer-governed irrigation systems.[71] The management of these systems was done through annual assemblies between local farmers and informally on a regular basis. Thus agreements for using the system, its monitoring, and sanctions for transgression were all done on a grassroots level. Ostrom noticed that farmer-governed irrigation systems were more likely to produce not in favor of markets, but for the needs of local communities, which grow more rice and distribute water more equitably. She concluded that although the systems in question vary in performance, few of them perform as poorly as the ones provided and managed by the state.

One of the brightest contemporary examples of reclaiming the commons is the Zapatista movement. Indigenous people of Chiapas, Mexico revolted in 1994 against the NAFTA agreement that was seeking the complete enclosure of common-pool resources and goods, vital for the livelihood of indigenous communities. Through the Zapatista uprising the locals reclaimed their land and resources and have been successfully managing them through a participatory system based on direct democracy for more than 25 years.

The digital commons, on the other hand, include wikis, such as Wikipedia, open licensing organizations, such as the Creative Commons, and many others. The social movement researcher Mayo Fuster Morell defines them as:

information and knowledge resources that are collectively created and owned or shared between or among a community and that tend to be non-exclusivedible, that is, be (generally freely) available to third parties. Thus, they are oriented to favor use and reuse, rather than toward exchange as a commodity. Additionally, the community of people building them can intervene in the governing of their interaction processes and of their shared resources.[72]

In other words, the logic of the commons is the striving toward inclusiveness and collective access to resources, knowledge, and other sources of collective wealth, which necessarily requires the creation of an anthropological type of socially active and devoted stewards of these commons. This means a radical break with the current dominant imaginary of economism, which views all human beings simply as rational materialists, always striving at maximizing their utilitarian self-interest. Instead, it implies a radical self-instituting of society which allows its citizens directly to manage their own commons.

The commons as model for the future

A main characteristic shared between the different cases of commons is the grassroots interactivity. The broad accessibility of such resources and their ownership being held in common by society, presupposes that their management is done by society itself. Thus state involvement is incompatible with such a broad popular self-management, since statist forms imply the establishment of bureaucratic managerial layers separated from society. That is, the commons go beyond (and are often even detrimental to) the various projects for nationalization.

The same goes for the constant neoliberal efforts of enclosing what's still not privatized, against which social movements across the globe have risen up, and their alternative proposals included in one form or another a wide project of direct democracy. It inevitably includes every sphere of social life, and that goes for the commons as well.

A holistic alternative to the contemporary system, that incorporates the project of direct democracy and the commons, can be drawn from the writings of great libertarian theorists such as Cornelius Castoriadis and Murray Bookchin. The proposals developed by the two thinkers offer an indispensable glimpse of how society can directly manage itself without and against external managerial mechanisms.

As we saw in the cases presented above, the commons require coordination between the commoners so eventual "tragedies" could be avoided. But for many, such as Knight and Merriam, this could possibly work only in small-scale cases. This has led many leftists to support different forms of state bureaucracy to manage the commons in the name of society, as the lesser, but possible, evil.

In his writings, Castoriadis repeatedly repudiated this hypothesis, claiming instead that large-scale collective decision-making is possible with a suitable set of tools and procedures and rejecting the idea of one correct model. His ideas were heavily influenced by the experience of ancient Athens. Drawing upon the Athenian *polis*, he claimed that direct citizen participation was possible in communities of up to 40,000 people.[73] On this level, communities can decide on matters that directly affect them in face-to-face meetings (general assemblies). For decisions that affect other communities as well, revocable, short-term delegates are being elected by the local assemblies to join regional councils. Through such a horizontal flow of collective power, common agreements and legal frameworks could be drawn to regulate and control the usage of commons.

Similar is the proposal made by Murray Bookchin. Also influenced by the ancient Athenian experience, he proposes the establishment of municipal face-to-face assemblies connected in democratic confederations, making the state apparatus obsolete. According to Bookchin, in such cases, "the control of the economy is not in the hands of the state, but under the custody of 'confederal councils,' and thus, neither collectivized nor privatized, it is common."[74]

Such a "nestedness" does not necessarily translate into hierarchy, as suggested by Elinor Ostrom and David Harvey,[75] at least if certain requirements are being met. As is the case in many of the practical examples of direct democracy around the world, the role of the delegates is of vital importance, but often neglected. Thus their subordination to the assemblies (as the main source of power) has to be asserted through various mechanisms, such as: short-term mandates, rotation, and selection by lot. All of these mechanisms have been tested in different times and contexts and have proven to be effective antidotes to the oligarchization of the political system.

Through such networking and self-instituting the direct control of commons by many communities that depend on them can be established. Another element that could supplement the propositions, described above, is the so-called solidarity economy. Spreading as mushrooms, different collective entities in different forms are rapidly spreading across Europe[76] and other crisis-stricken areas (such as South America) allowing communities to directly manage their economic activities in their favor.

One such merger will allow society to collectively draw the set of rules which regulate the usage of the commons, while solidarity economic entities, such as cooperatives and collectives, will advance the commons' direct management. These entities are being managed through direct democracy by the people working in them who will be rewarded in a dignified manner for their services by the attended communities. On the other hand, the public deliberative institutions should have mechanisms for supervision and control over the solidarity economic entities responsible for the management of commons in order to prevent any moves toward privatization.

One example for such merging has occurred in the Bolivian city of Santa Cruz where the water management is organized in the form of a consumer cooperative.[77] It has been functioning for more than 20 years, and continues to enjoy a reputation as one of the best-managed utilities in Latin America. The cooperative is being governed by a General Delegate Assembly elected by the users. The assembly appoints senior management over whom the users have veto rights, thus perpetuating stability.

This model has drastically reduced corruption, making the water system functional for the consumers.

The emergence of such a merger between the commons and the cooperative production of value, as Michel Bauwens and Vasilis Kostakis suggest,[78] serves to integrate externalities, practice economic democracy, produce commons for the common good, and socialize its knowledge. The circulation of the commons would be combined with the process of cooperative accumulation on behalf of the commons and its contributors. In such a model the logic of free contribution and universal use for everyone would coexist with directly democratic networking and a cooperative mode of physical production based upon the principle of reciprocity.

Conclusion

The need to recreate the commons is an urgent one. With global instability still on the horizon and deepening, the question of how we will share our common world is the thin line separating the dichotomous world of market barbarity and bureaucratic heteronomy from a possible world based upon collective and individual autonomy. As Hannah Arendt argued:

The public realm, as the common world, gathers us together and yet prevents our falling over each other, so to speak. What makes mass society so difficult to bear is not the number of people involved, or at least not primarily, but the fact that the world between them has lost its power to gather them together, to relate and to separate them. The weirdness of this situation resembles a spiritualistic séance where a number of people gathered around a table might suddenly, through some magic trick, see the table vanish from their midst, so that two persons sitting opposite each other were no longer separated but also would be entirely unrelated to each other by anything tangible.[79]

The paradigm of the commons, as part of the wider project of direct democracy, could play the role of the trick that manages to vanish the table separating us, but simultaneously create strong human relationships based on solidarity and participation. For this to happen, social movements and communities have to reclaim the public space and the commons. This occurs through the establishment of networks and the strengthening of already existing ones, thus constituting a coherent counterpower and creating real possibilities of instituting in practice new forms of social organization beyond state and markets.

Degrowth: Exposing the Fallacy of Unlimited Economic Growth

The insistence on work and production is a malign one.
Giorgio Agamben[80]

We are told that we need still more economic growth in order to overcome the present multi-layer crises. Actually, we have been hearing this for quite some time now. Both right and left, capitalist and socialist governments, offer their theories about how we need more production and consumption in order for our societies to progress and overcome the present difficulties.

The narrative of constant economic growth

But a question arises – isn't our economy already more than big enough? Our production and consumption levels are already outgrowing our planet's biocapacity by nearly 60 per cent each year.[81] Constantly expanding, material extraction and consumption on a global scale have peaked at almost 70 billion tonnes annually.[82] And the current projections show that this rapid growth will continue – it is expected that by the year 2100 we will be producing three times more waste than we do today.[83]

This constant process of large-scale resource extraction and consumption has triggered a severe degradation of nature. Scientists are warning that we are witnessing the greatest mass extinction of species in more than 65 million years.[84] Due to human economic activity a climate change has been set in motion (with each year passing being hotter than the previous) that threatens to trigger large-scale displacement of people (climate refugees). In many parts of the world soil fertility is being degraded by GMO crops while water and air are being polluted to levels dangerous for human health. Whole islands consisting of garbage are being formed above the deepest points of our oceans.[85] The list goes on and on. Having said this, we can go as far as to talk of a war on nature.

It is not clear how we will be able to reverse the ecological crisis provoked by the Anthropocene if we continue down the same path. The global leaders admit the problem and call for keeping CO_2 emissions down, in order to keep within the "below 2 degrees Celsius" goal,[86] while paradoxically insisting on more resource extraction, industrial production, long-distance shipment, and consumption.

According to the dominant narrative, we need economic growth even at the price of irreversible ecological catastrophe in order to cope with inequality and poverty. Here another question arises – with the growth already achieved until now we should have made some significant progress in this direction, shouldn't we have?

Instead, in most contemporary societies, despite their growing economies, there is an increase in inequality. According to Jason Hickel from the London School of Economics, the world's richest 1 per cent have increased their profits by 60 per cent in the last 20 years,[87] during which time global economic inequality was rapidly rising – a period of constant economic growth on a global scale.

This is so because economic growth does not indicate general social wellbeing. If a few bankers get much richer, the indicator of average income can go up, even as the income of most individuals declines. The growing indebtedness can also potentially contribute to economic growth as was the case with Ireland before it descended into crisis. For example, if the incomes of slum dwellers rise, it will be an insignificant gain for the economic sector, whereas the same does not apply for the richest strata of society, whose expanding piece of the economic pie consists mostly of the global economy.

These negative effects of the doctrine of constant economic growth were already noticed in 1897 by Errico Malatesta, who in his book *At the Café* wrote:

These evils [social inequality, poverty, unemployment] generally are more intense in countries where the industry is more developed, except if the workers themselves didn't manage, through organizing at the working place, resistance or revolt, to achieve better living conditions.[88]

The paradigm of fair growth

The European Left (as was the case with the Greek SYRIZA Party when in power during the period 2015-2019[89]) has been advancing the promise of sharing the "pie" in a more just manner. But still, as if it is not already big enough, it must grow further. It is unclear why this should happen and why we cannot share the plenty we already have. Is the ruling Left merely trying to buy itself more time in power?

The European proposal of "left-winged" growth is based on the so-called *progressivismo* of Latin America, where supposedly progressive governments have conducted large-scale extractivist policies in order to improve the general wellbeing of society. Despite the obvious ecological costs such projects usually have, it's also worth noticing the negative effects they have on rural and indigenous communities[90]. By the enclosure and commodification of common-pool resources which accompany the extractivist policies, traditionally sustainable ways of life are made practically impossible, thus forcing the members of these communities to search for wage-based livelihoods in megalopolises, often ending up in the urban slums.

For the enrichment of the metropolitan middle and upper classes, sustainable ways of life are being sacrificed. And what are they being sacrificed for? For a life of increasing dependence in an unhealthy environment. That's why much of the critique and resistance against the pink-tide in Latin America came from those located at the bottom of the pyramid – the indigenous communities, the first that are being sacrificed in the name of so-called progress.

We can assume therefore that economic growth is incompatible with ecological and self-sustainable ways of life. In order to continue growing, the modern economy needs to absorb as much of the commons as possible, making impossible human interactions outside of it. Some, such as Google and Facebook, the two fastest-growing corporations in the history of capitalism, are going as far as to commodify our very existence in the datascape, squeezing our digital life for surplus value.[91] And by doing this, economic growth actually strengthens the capitalist system, which is, alongside the state apparatus, responsible for the deepening social inequalities.

Thus the Left's promise that constant economic growth could lower the current levels of inequality and poverty is at least unrealistic. On the one hand, it is a promise toward the many that are in need and stricken by the crisis. On the other – toward the richest strata, promising them that the current social imbalances will not be disturbed.

But even if somehow a reduction of poverty and inequality is achieved in the distant future through constant economic growth, it will be at the price of irreversible environmental damage that will affect human health such as the unbreathable air of the Chinese megalopolises, or the inflammable water in American towns where shale-gas fracking is taking place. But there will be a cost also on the socio-political level. In this process self-sufficient and democratic ways of life will be sacrificed and absorbed by unstable capitalist entities and the states that strive to commodify and bureaucratize everything. Thus alternative approaches will be pushed even further away from the social imaginary.

Overcoming economism: toward direct democracy and ecology

Instead, we should abandon the growth doctrine altogether and direct our attention toward the already enormous pace of economic production. There is no point in enlarging it even further; on the contrary, if we want to have any future on this planet, we will have to de-grow it. But this can have meaning only if we decide to share it equally. And this cannot be done by the state or other hierarchical extra-social structures, for equality requires equal participation in the decision-making by all citizens. Thus here we speak for a major paradigm change: an altogether abandonment of the capitalist economism of *Homo economicus* and embracing of the social ecology of active citizens, impassioned about public affairs and conscious of their symbiotic relationship with nature.

This implies that instead of elected representatives, economic oligarchs or artificial economic indicators to determine where the pieces of the economic "pie" should go, this should be done by interconnected direct-democratic institutions like popular assemblies and councils of revocable delegates that give the opportunity for direct participation to every member of society. In her field work in the US, Guatemala, Kenya, Turkey, Nepal, and elsewhere, Nobel-prize recipient Elinor Ostrom observed[92] similar patterns of communal management of commons that didn't merely avoid a theoretical tragedy but actually appeared quite sustainable.

In such a way, actual social, individual, and environmental needs, reflected by the above-mentioned deliberative bodies, will direct the size and purpose of economic activity. That way, already existing and functioning technologies could be put to serve people and nature, reducing the work day and creating more time for creativity, philosophy, politics, art, and enjoyment. Energy could be acquired through decentralized and renewable means, fostering local self-sufficiency and sustainability. Tools and devices could be made long-lasting by designing them to be upgradable rather than replaceable. All these and many more are already possible with the current state of our development.

The rejection of economic growth does not mean a retreat to primitivism, but rather a different use and understanding of what we already have and will acquire in the future. Scientific researches and experiments needn't stop taking place, but they shouldn't be navigated by the economism of short-term profits for the few, but by the general commonwealth of people and nature. And this includes conscious self-limitation, that is, the possibility of society itself to decide in a deliberative manner which directions to progress in, and what technology (or knowledge) should be treated with caution, or even restrained.

Here it is worth noticing that the technological progress that is being praised by the advocates of capitalism and economic growth is, quite possibly, not their strongest side. In his book *Utopia of Rules*, David Graeber points to the unfulfilled popular hopes of technological miracles we should have acquired by now. Instead, the imperatives of constant economic growth, bureaucratic hierarchy, and short-term market competitiveness have made companies and scientists indulge mainly in developing information technologies,[93] that is, technologies of simulation, or what Jean Baudrillard and Umberto Eco call "hyper-real" – the ability to make imitations more realistic than the original. Thus real progress in this field was replaced by a spectacle.

Grassroots resistance to economic growth

As is obvious from what's been said above, this democratic paradigm is not confined to the economy. Instead, it encompasses all spheres of human life and their relation to nature, offering a holistic and sustainable vision for our future, based on symbiotic, rather than competitive, relations between people, and between humanity and nature. And it cannot but be enforced from the bottom-up – in a non-statist, anti-capitalist, direct-democratic, ecological manner.

We can already see that in many parts of the world projects aimed at enforcing economic growth are being met with hostility by local communities. From India's farmers burning GMO crops, which are degrading their land, to indigenous and environmental groups in the US that have managed during the last couple of years to stop some mega-projects – including the Keystone XL and the North Dakota[94] pipelines that were supposed to transfer large quantities of oil across drinkable water sources, putting in danger water quality and the lives of the locals.

But even in the countries that can be considered pioneers of the "Fair Growth" concept we see such reactions. In Bolivia *comunarios* (communal peasants)[95] are protesting against the government's extremely extractivist policies that are contributing to the warming of the climate and the drought that impoverishes local farmers. In Ecuador, indigenous and ecological movements have gained such a momentum that President Correa's administration went as far as to criminalize environmental activism classifying it as terrorism.[96]

We can conclude that economic growth, either Right or Left-wing, cannot solve the present social problems. Instead it strengthens capitalism and statist hierarchies, which only deepen the roots of the present crisis. For them to be successfully tackled, a completely different paradigm is needed, one that will not aim at cursory "fix-ups," but will deal with the real causes of our problems in a holistic manner. We all need to support and participate in such struggles and movements by connecting them with each other, introducing them to alternatives like decentralizing power, putting it back in the hands of interconnected local communities, and making all of us conscious of our dependence on nature.

Solidarity Economy as a Revolutionary Strategy

The solidarity economy proposes more transparency, much more democracy, much more participation, much more redistribution of wealth and goods of production. The solidarity economy fights for free software, for free knowledge, for freedom of access to information, completely.
Beverly Bell and Jessica Hsu[97]

In a sense the so-called solidarity economy has always existed in one form or another. Many thinkers were interested in it and themselves developed theories that contributed to its development: people such as Beatrice Webb, Charles Fourier, Robert Owen, and many more. But various forms that can be assumed as typical for the solidarity economy, such as sharing, barter, and non-intermediary producer-consumer relations, organized through direct participation and equality, were present in various historic moments in the everyday life of humanity from ancient times.

According to Pierre Clastres[98] in primitive societies the people controlled their own actions and the circulation of products deriving from them. In these societies production is measured according to needs that have to be satisfied. When their needs are satisfied, the so-called primitive people did not strive to produce more, that is, to alienate their time by working for no reason, instead filling it with creativity, rest, fun, and thinking.

Afterwards we can point at the guild economies that emerged in the medieval European cities. According to Peter Kropotkin,[99] the guilds set common economic rules, but they themselves were based on different interests. The medieval guilds were unities of people sharing the same occupation (traders, producers, artisans, for example), regardless of their status: master or apprentice. Each guild was sovereign in its sphere, but couldn't alone by itself take decisions regarding the rest of the guilds. That's why they formed federations through which collectively to determine the rules of the ongoing economic processes in society.

In recent years considerable interest toward the solidarity economy was experienced in many countries across Latin America. There, during the 1980s, the solidarity economy was established as terms and set of practices.[100] But the number of people involved in it continued to increase during the next decade, as a result of the economic crises[101] tearing the continent, as well as the spreading consumerist culture, stripping human life of meaning. Thus the people involved with practices that could be attributed to the solidarity economy didn't have a homogenous character but were coming from different milieux of life: from poor families to middle- and upper-middle class ones. All of them helped the creation of many producer and consumer cooperatives, community associations, and collective kitchens.

In 1998, in the Brazilian city of Porto Alegre, famous for its system of participatory budgeting, there was a convening of the "Latin American Solidarity Economy Network." Participants in it were activists from all over the continent and even Europe: Brazil, Mexico, Argentina, Peru, Nicaragua, Bolivia, Colombia, and Spain. The commonalities between their practices are many: the striving toward justice, creativity, self-management, and autonomy.

Henceforth, the solidarity economy became an international movement. During the first World Social Forum in 2001 the Global Network of the Solidarity Socioeconomy was established. By 2004 it was already including networks from over 47 countries from all over the world, that is, tens of thousands of democratic economic initiatives.

From 2008 onwards the solidarity economy started flourishing across Europe, boosted to a large degree by the economic crisis which hit all European social stratas. Especially in countries like Greece and Spain, the combination of, on the one hand, high levels of unemployment, and on the other, long traditions of resistance and self-organization led to the creation of thousands of horizontal economic structures covering a wide spectrum of services which provided for the livelihood of growing amounts of people with different social status and ideas.

Solidarity economy versus social economy

Quite often the solidarity economy is being mistaken for social economy. There are, however, significant differences between the practices and the very logic between the two of them.[102]

The social economy usually signifies the third sector of the economy, which plays a subsidiary role to the first, which is private, for profit, and the second, which is statist. The definitions of what the social economy is may vary, but there are certain commonalities among them that help us form a general idea; it is a sector based on cooperatives, associations, and non-governmental organizations, which have rather collective characters and prioritize social goals rather than increasing profits. This does not mean that, in reality, it's not realizing profits needed for reinvestment and maintenance.

At the core of the logic behind the social economy is the idea of covering the gaps that the present system is unable to cover for one or another reason. In a sense it can be viewed as a third pillar of capitalism together with the private and the state sectors. In accordance with this logic, those involved in the social economy often resort to and depend on various charitable foundations and state programs, seeing in them potential allies.

The solidarity economy, on the other hand, is rooted in a much different paradigm based on direct democracy, equality, and mutual aid.[103] Thus it is incompatible with and antagonistic to the dominant politico-economic model of top-down bureaucratic decision-making and competition (social cannibalism). It strives for the complete replacement of the state-private dichotomy. The solidarity economy opposes the very doctrine of constant economic growth on which capitalism is based, and proposes in its place not a retreat to the stronger state of the past, which is also based on the same growth doctrine, but the establishment of autonomous communities which democratically determine their needs instead of using some artificial market mechanisms for greater synergy to be achieved between humanity and nature.

What differentiates the solidarity economy from other movements for social change and revolutionary currents is its pluralist approach – it refutes the idea of one sole and correct road and instead recognizes that there are multiple practices, many of which are rooted in antiquity. Its target is not the creation of one utopia from scratch, but to locate and connect the many mini-utopias, germs of new worlds, already emerging and existing around us. The solidarity economy places the person at the heart of the economy, thus the direct citizen participation and the establishment of solidarian relationships based on trust play a central role in it.

All this indicates that the solidarity economy has a completely transformational, anti-capitalist, and non-statist character, whereas the social economy deals with contemporary injustices in the frames of the state and the capitalist market, striving to reform and humanize capitalism.

Main characteristics

What we call labour has not the slightest resemblance to a commodity. It is simply an aspect of man's life, which is neither detachable from him, nor capable of being hoarded, or transported, or manufactured, or consumed.
Karl Polanyi[104]

Beyond economism

Nowadays, the social imaginary is successfully being modeled in the framework of economism. We can say that everything is being subjected to the economy and its basic engine – the paradigm of constant growth. Local communities, the nation-states, and entire populations as well as nature are being subjected to the will of the "almighty" markets. Our habitats in cities and homes as well as the way we think are being narrowed along economism's basic principles: hierarchy, alienation, and competition or social cannibalism.

However, many on the Left entrap themselves in the narrative imposed on us by the authorities through all the tools they have at their disposal – media, educational systems, police, and others – that the contemporary politico-economic model is extremely decentralized, if not "anarchic." Thus many leftists oppose its chaotic nature by proposing a return to the big bureaucratic governments of the past. But if we inspect the dominant system more carefully, we will see that this narrative is merely a cover masking an equally authoritarian and centralized model of decision-making with transnational financial and economic institutions dictating the political direction of entire societies.

The domination of this logic of hegemony of the economic over the political is being absorbed by society. The most common way of life, as we can observe it in every contemporary capitalist nation-state, is based on mindless consumption and alienating individualism. Resistance toward the dominant order, since it emerges from the midst of this very culture, remains entrapped in an economically-centered way of thinking: for a long time the alternative economic demands and models were among the top priorities of activists worldwide.

The paradigm of the solidarity economy represents a radical break with economism. Although it ostensibly seems like just another economic model, it goes much further than this. First of all, by placing the political question of inclusive and participatory forms of decision-making at its core, solidarity economy is embedding itself into a wider project of direct democracy which encompasses all spheres of human life and nature, placing above all the political question of who determines the way of life and how they do it. Thus it cannot be viewed separately from wider social and environmental emancipation.

The very practices of solidarity economy are much more rooted in social deliberation and communitarian relationships rather than the narrow questions of production and consumption which also tend to be charged with ethical and political characteristics.

Ecology

In accordance with the worldview of economism, nature is viewed as a mere commodity that can be injected into service for economic growth. Forests are being rapidly cut, water basins are being depleted, animal species are disappearing at a scary haste, not to mention resources such as oil. In a few words, everything is being commodified, and the question being posed is not if, but when and how.

The very development of our societies is being presented as hostile toward nature. Usually this indicates more jobs, more cars and technology, which, according to today's dominant logic, requires overexploitation of nature. This worldview is being shared by many on the Left as well, being rooted in the same growth-based, anthropocentric logic.

We can detect, in the root of this worldview, the logic of domination, of hierarchy or power and control. The idea of human domination over nature is the same one of human domination over other humans. Thus is the principle of hierarchy that is located at the heart of our present-day ecological crisis.

However, the typical approaches toward the preservation of nature do not seem to reach this conclusion. Most people view nature as a commodity completely in accordance with the dominant imaginary. Thus their demands circulate around the preservation of certain limited areas which are then to be exploited for tourism. In economic terms, the equivalent of it is the so-called green capitalism which includes certain state involvement in the economy and environmentally "responsible" behavior by capitalist firms. These exploitative economies do not challenge the economic hierarchies and the very concept of constant growth.

Unlike the pseudo-ecological approaches just described, the solidarity economy challenges both the growth doctrine and the hierarchical economic relations. Its target is not constant over-production and articulation of artificial needs in the name of profits for the few (economic growth). On the contrary, it aims at satisfying the needs of everyone involved in it through the mechanisms of common ownership and direct-democratic managerial procedures. The direct participation at its core ensures that the needs, created and satisfied by the solidarity economy, are real individual and communal needs, and not captured by bureaucrats or corporate CEOs.

As a result, the solidarity economy does not seek to exploit nature, but on the contrary, strives to nurture it, since the people and communities at the grassroots depend on their land, forests, fisheries, and other services provided by nature. By rejecting the logic of domination of humans over other humans, it, sometimes consciously and sometimes not, also repudiates the domination of humans over nature. This is ever-more evident from the adoption of ecologic practices (such as permaculture) by many collectives and cooperatives from solidarity economy networks in their production and services.

Beyond state and free market

Countless practices in all spheres of human life, including the economic one, which mainly interests us here, are successfully existing beyond and antagonistic to statist bureaucracies and capitalist markets. The contemporary ruling elites, however, have interest in the hegemony of the latter two, thus harnessing all their powers toward the promotion of the market-state nexus as the only valid and realistic one. The mainstream narrative today has successfully been hijacked by this false dilemma which influences the direction of the dominant politics as well as their presupposed alternatives.

On the one hand there is the capitalist model with its private sector, "free" market, and constant economic growth. Nowadays these are the most powerful forces influencing politics and social relations. However, they are one of the main sources of desperation and misery. By the enclosure of common resources by private owners, many people are left without anything but their bare hands to sell their labor power to the landlords. Even the societies in the so-called first world are suffering from the effects of the capitalist system. The consumerist culture and corporate hierarchy enforced by it are stripping everyday life of meaning and dignity, while economic growth, as the main engine of capitalism, destroys the environment and makes it hazardous for people's health.

The market-state pseudo-dilemma suggests that the sole alternative to market-based capitalism is a state-based pseudo-socialism (state capitalism). But a closer look at the latter shows why this is a pseudo-dilemma. In its essence the state is a hierarchical and bureaucratic mechanism that encloses common resources and then assigns functionaries to manage them for the society without allowing social participation. Thus it once again deprives society of its direct interaction with its environment and introduces a tiny managerial elite which in practice is the owner by having the last word about how things should be done.

The solidarity economy is cutting across this pseudo-dilemma, proposing instead direct management of the economy by those involved in it: individuals and their communities. The direct-democratic procedures and collective-communal forms of ownership it incorporates exclude the private owners as well as the state and party functionaries. Thus the control of the economy is placed into the hands of society itself. This is evident from the incompatibility that practices of solidarity economy are showing toward the state and the capitalist business as I noted in the previous chapter. That's why it is important – and often is being done – for the solidarity economy to be incorporated into a holistic project of direct democracy which will be able to challenge the domination of the capitalist market as well as that of the state in all spheres of life.

Beyond determinism

Determinism is one of the main pillars of economism. Thus our current capitalist system, as well as the totalitarian socialist one of the past (state capitalism), is built on it. Economic determinism is based on the idea that a pseudoscience can exist to calculate the human potential and predict the direction humanity will take in the future. In a sense it is a kind of mythology which creates a certain narrative, excluding some practices and logics, while presenting other ones as realistic and possible.

It is a precondition for the contemporary dominant market-state nexus for which I wrote previously. The "free" market and the state are configured in certain historical stages which can vary according to different economic and deterministic theories but are necessary conditions for the further advancement of humanity. Thus they are being viewed by experts, economists, and politicians as the only systems that are possible, real, and rational. In this way third alternative organizational forms are being excluded as utopian, that is, maybe desirable in a naïve way but completely impractical and foolish.

The solidarity economy, as opposed to the imaginary of economism, goes well beyond this deterministic logic. It does not pretend that it knows what it should do tomorrow in terms of a tight politico-economic program. That's why it encompasses different economic forms, varying in certain aspects, but always sharing democratic and collaborative principles.

The solidarity economy can be viewed as a tool for experimenting in real time, rather than a strict economic model. Exactly because it does not rest on deterministic thinking, it experiments from today with different practices that share some desirable principles, trying to discover their advantages and disadvantages, in order to develop them further or engage with new ones that appear in the processes. The solidarity economy thus fits with the famous slogan, raised by the Zapatistas: *We walk while asking*.

From externalization to internalization of the economy

The final characteristic to which I will direct attention in this chapter is the way the economy is being viewed through the paradigm of solidarity economy. This question, of course, is tightly connected with economism and determinism.

In mainstream economics, economy is viewed as something separated from society, a science that calculates the social dynamics and produces models that people should follow. This logic is a fertile soil for the emergence of technocratic elites of experts, who know what the economy is, how it operates, and thus, should direct the rest of society – the great majority of it – which is considered to be unenlightened in the mysteries of economics. Thus the dominant hierarchical organizational structure of society is not only maintained but deepened even further.

The solidarity economy represents a radical break with this logic. By embedding the economic practices it encompasses into the everyday life of the participant individuals and communities, it manages to integrate the economy into the whole of society, thus making obsolete the role of technocrats and experts who feed on its externalization. In a sense, it dissolves the economy into autonomous economic practices which can be experimented with and changed separately unlike large-scale models such as capitalism and state "socialism."

Thus the solidarity economy creates the opportunity for different expressions of popular anger and dissatisfaction with the status quo, unlike the forms of resistance that have dominated the revolutionary movements for centuries, such as electing so-called radical governments, fighting over the seats of power, or trying to destroy every last bit of the present system so as to start anew. The solidarity economy offers a different paradigm. It allows people to express it through creativity by building new forms of production and consumption relationships, based on the fundamentally different core principles and goals of direct democracy, trust, solidarity, and dignity.

Solidarity economy as transformational strategy

The public, the people, will find a way to create forms we cannot even imagine, forms that could solve problems that seem insuperable to us. So what is needed is this constant creative activity from the public, and that means mainly everybody's passion for public affairs.
Cornelius Castoriadis[105]

The solidarity economy, as I have already underlined earlier, is directly linked to direct democracy in actuality because at its core are direct participation and cooperation. But in order to move these principles from the margins of our collective life toward its center we need first to deeply democratize ourselves.

The implementation of direct democracy on larger scales is impossible without the wider self-empowerment of common people (those situated "below"). In the end who will realize in practice one system, based on popular participation, if not the individual and society itself? Who will participate in the direct-democratic institutions we imagine if not the people themselves?

This requires a strategy for inclusive self-empowerment or, in other words, changing the anthropological type of the modern human. Surely one such project will demand a lot of time and effort simultaneously on a practical and theoretical level which will allow people to develop democratic habits and culture. This is something highly neglected by classic ideological movements.

It is important to note here that people will not start suddenly to cooperate, share, and participate directly in the management of their collective life, as if this is embedded in their DNA. In critical situations society does not have time to develop brand new solutions; on the contrary, it turns desperately toward already existing structures, even if they are established on a small scale, and toward political proposals that may have been hidden from the eye, but never completely vanished. As Cornelius Castoriadis warns us about the moments of disappointment and social crisis, when the consciousness of society grows rapidly:

> But to be socially effective – this autonomous mass action cannot remain amorphous, fragmented, and dispersed. It will find expression in patterns of action and forms of organization, in ways of doing things and ultimately in institutions which embody and reflect its purpose...If libertarian revolutionaries remain blissfully unaware of these problems and have not discussed or even envisaged them they can rest assured that others have.[106]

Thus if we want one day to live in a non-hierarchical society, based on solidarity and direct democracy, we will have to create the necessary conditions for its existence.

In other words, if we want values like solidarity and self-management to take a central place in our lives, we will need people who are embracing them deeply. We will need many of them. And since our contemporary culture does not have such priorities, it will be necessary to find other ways of opening spaces in which to plant the seeds, as bearers of different cultures. Good examples for such spaces are the autonomous zones, functioning all around the world inside urban areas, as well as those on a larger scale, such as the Zapatistas and the Kurdish democratic communities.

Everything in the contemporary organization of our society obstructs such principles, inculcating instead submission and obedience toward authority and heteronomous acceptance of predetermined truths. This is the situation in the modern family, state apparatus, corporate workplace, education, and other social domains.

We derive our education in classrooms in which our attention is focused on the figure of the teacher who is positioned "above" students. Horizontal interaction between students during class is overtly punished. From an early age our imaginary is being framed and our creativity is dulled by established norms which sustain the existing hierarchical culture. We are being taught to "think" in a "correct" way, so we can "win" the school competition, by giving the "right" answers to the teacher's questions. A whole set of punishments and sanctions simultaneously function for the students and teachers that dare to drift away from the top-down norm.

Another negative aspect, which grows out of this type of relationship, is that the great majority today thinks only about how to get a job instead of how to live in a meaningful manner. By thinking in this narrow careerist paradigm, people begin to view all their life as a constant interaction between bosses and employees without any concept of alternatives. In one such mindset there is no (or very limited) space for principles such as direct democracy, cooperation, and solidarity. But in reality this paradigm dominates the imaginary of the majority of people working in every economic sector all around the world with tiny exceptions.

If the situation nowadays is such, what will happen with our principles and our desire to spread them across? In my opinion, to have any success in this direction social movements are needed in which we participate to generate cooperative and direct-democratic power. And this can happen mainly through common people that deeply value these principles. But how will our horizontal movements achieve this? What will lead to such change in the anthropological type so as to move beyond the imaginary of the passive consumer and to charge it with a protagonistic role in the public sphere?

Surely the answer to these questions is not an easy one. One strategy for this is the transformation on a small scale, at the local level, simultaneously in coordination with other similar processes taking place elsewhere. Here I will briefly sketch the strategy of the solidarity economy and a narrative which can help us in this direction.

The solidarity economy as practice, vision, and strategy is not something new and a growing number of people are practicing it, especially after the global financial crisis in 2008. At first sight it may not seem that difficult to implement, but in fact it is quite a task: to develop a new anthropological type, communities, local organizations, and networks, that can turn solidarity economy into an important and unavoidable part of the economic processes in society.

In order for this to happen, we will have to practice it to such a degree and with such success that common people will be able to recognize it by its basic characteristics. Reaching larger scales depends on the collaboration between various initiatives from the solidarity economy, such as workers and consumers cooperatives, time banks, social currencies, and housing cooperatives. Their success depends as much on the collaboration between them, as well as on their inner organization – the maintenance of democratic procedures through various mechanisms such as rotation of positions, distribution of profits among members according to effort, and personal sacrifice.

There are disagreements and debates among the supporters of this vision about what is to be done for its practical realization. In my opinion, this project is infeasible if we consider it only in terms of generations, neglecting our lives here and now. I make this claim because many people are managing to bring more autonomy into their everyday life in different parts of the world, including Spain, Greece, Brazil, and India. However, we shouldn't abandon the generational prism completely because many struggles of the past have sown the seeds of ways of life which are coming to life today. The achievement of this goal can be accomplished through a strategy for the development of culture, which can spread beyond narrow economic and social frames. By making this claim we acknowledge that people are economic and social beings, as well as sexual and, beyond all, political ones.

Thus among the main goals of the solidarity economy should be the constant connection of self-managed economic units across various economic sectors. In such a way could be sought the establishment of regional networks for sustainable long-term development of relations of production and consumption. The culmination of this inclusiveness should be sought through the establishment of networks of solidarity economies across the world for the satisfaction of an ever-growing amount of human needs through autonomous and democratic means, challenging the very existence of statist and capitalist intermediaries.

For such a project to be completed, however, it should overcome the limitations of economism. As I have shown earlier, in its essence, the solidarity economy is part of a wider direct-democratic political project and thus should have to engage in close collaboration with social movements of different kinds. In this way the efforts to introduce more autonomy in the economic relations in society will go along with similar efforts directed at ecology, gender, and other crises.

Thus we can say that the solidarity economy is focused on the creation of another type of culture starting today, in the shell of the dominant system, without depending on the state and the private sector. Through this process the self-empowerment of the involved individuals and communities is encouraged, and simultaneously we are offered practical examples for how solidarity and collaboration can become the basic significational framework of the economy.

In other words, the solidarity economy can serve as a tool for dealing with the cultural challenge by teaching us how to create spaces which could help us rethink our values as they are today, those that are making us apathetic consumers. Such a step could open the possibility for people to become protagonists in their life by deeply democratizing them and their environment, moving principles such as solidarity and direct participation out of the margins and toward the center of our collective and individual lives.[107]

These new principles and values stemming from the grassroots can replace the current dominant trends toward consumerism and hierarchy. But the political manifestoes and ready blueprints for the future are not sufficient preconditions for this to happen. They have to begin penetrating every sphere of our life. The solidarity economy as a transformational strategy can make us more independent from the contemporary dominant structures, thus allowing us to begin the creation of alternative post-capitalist and non-statist futures.

Citizen Participation as Antidote to Social Paranoia

Before they seize power and establish a world according to their doctrines, totalitarian movements conjure up a lying world of consistency which is more adequate to the needs of the human mind than reality itself.
Hannah Arendt[108]

Conspiracy theories seem to be gaining momentum and have even led people out onto the streets to protest. "9/11 was an inside-job" believers, flat Earthers, anti-vaxxers, Covid-19 skeptics, and Qanon followers – the crowd of conspiracy theorists appears to be growing. Many tend to blame this phenomenon on the low education of those who believe in such ideas.[109] Others openly call for the further technocratization of politics as solution to this trend.[110]

But vesting technocrats with more power is actually part of the problem. There is another factor that drives this rise of conspiracy theories – disempowerment. Psychology professor Jan-Willem van Prooijen, in a research paper, traces various sources that indicate how when "people feel powerless, or experience a lack of control over their environment, they are more likely to believe conspiracy theories."[111] The Association for Psychological Science has reached a similar conclusion: "A recent review of the scientific literature on conspiracy theories indicates that these ideas may appeal to people trying to make sense in a world that leaves them feeling disempowered, alienated, and confused."[112]

There seems to be much logic in that explanation as people have become justifiably suspicious of authorities. Contemporary technocrats and experts are part of a lineage that claimed its right to rule over society that dates far back into human history, in particular the practice of gerontocracy.

Murray Bookchin sites the latter, along with patriarchy, as the foundational base of social hierarchies, domination, and exploitation.[113] It was the elders, usually male, who claimed to possess knowledge and wisdom, that were beyond the reach of the rest of society. Thus together with the emerging warrior class, they began taking control over their fellow human beings.

Today the governing institutions continue this line of thought. It is no longer the oldest in society, but it is still the supposedly wisest and most knowledgeable who are elected to take charge of our lives. And in the meantime the rest of society is continuously distanced further away from the centers of power. No wonder, then, that people are increasingly suspicious of what the government, its experts, and the mainstream media are telling them. It is not that they have suddenly become irrational or anti-science, it's merely that they have been lied to too many times by institutions that were initially designed to maintain the privileged position of the ruling elites.

Unfortunately this distrust is most often being channeled through the dominant imaginary of capitalism and national discourse. Instead of reaching out to other disempowered citizens and attempting to change the political architecture, people who believe in conspiracy theories often fall into a state of collective narcissism – a belief that one's own social group is superior, but unappreciated – by other people as outlined in a recent report.[114] People who believe in conspiracy theories almost always view themselves as part of a people whose rightful place on top of society has been snatched away by someone else. In this way they don't move beyond the dominant imaginary that has disempowered them in the first place; they firmly participate in it.

It is no wonder then that researchers have suggested that "people immersed in conspiracy beliefs are less inclined to take actions that, in the long run, might boost their autonomy and control."[115] They are, instead, much more prone to prove their superiority over other groups. Michael Albert has argued that "conspiracy theories provide an easy and quick outlet for pent up passion withheld from targets that seem unassailable or that might strike back," which he concludes, "is downright conspiracy theory turned into scapegoat theory."[116] In this sense, conspiracy theories are deeply reactionary and in line with totalitarian tendencies.

In order for the wave of irrational and anti-scientific conspiracies to be tackled in any meaningful way, people collectively must be empowered to control their own lives. As van Prooijen suggests, this approach "might be more effective than trying to rationally refute conspiracy theories" because "many conspiracy theories are not rational to begin with, and moreover, rational reasoning is often not the root cause of conspiracy theories."[117]

If people have an opportunity to directly participate in the decision-making that determines the course of their societies, instead of being treated like infants, there will be little room left for fears of others secretly ruling over us. In one such setting, based on direct democracy, there will be no elites ruling society, nor closed expert groups hoarding knowledge, where information and science are made freely available to the public and not channeled through bureaucratic and/or for-profit institutions for the latter to be able to engage in rational and secular deliberation.

As author Joseph E. Uscinski has written in his book *Conspiracy Theories and the People Who Believe Them*:

If feelings of powerlessness increase belief in conspiracy theories, might the reverse also be true—that is, do feelings of empowerment decrease belief in conspiracy theories? Empowerment refers to the feeling that one is in control over one's own life, and can influence relevant decisions that shape one's future. Just like feelings of powerlessness are related with negative emotions, including fear, anxiety, and uncertainty, feelings of empowerment are likely to decrease such negative emotions and instead foster hope, optimism, and confidence in the future. Such positive emotions may stimulate citizens to perceive their social environment in a less suspicious state of mind.[118]

Such genuine empowerment, however, can be implemented only by society itself. No institution intended to preserve the privileges of an elite will willingly disperse its power among all of the population. It is the latter who must self-organize and radically alter the political architecture of society. In this endeavor conspiracy theories are nothing less than a great obstacle, and as such they must actively be resisted by the social movements. A more democratic and much less paranoid society is not only a viable alternative to the current alienating and authoritarian regime but a matter of social participation and organizing in the here-and-now.

In Defense of Popular Self-Governance

First of all, direct democracy, the democratic regime I'm thinking about, is not paradise on Earth.
It's not the perfect regime, and I don't know what perfect regime means.
Cornelius Castoriadis[119]

With the electoral successes in recent times of the far-right in Europe and around the world, certain fears of society – of the masses – have been resurrected among liberals and leftists, if such fears were ever dead. They are rooted in an elitist tradition shared by many political tendencies that view society as inherently irresponsible, if not even cannibalistic, and thus in need of restraint by enlightened extra-social institutions which keep it civilized.

This statist logic opens one deeply Hobbesian dilemma for us to choose between having individual liberties or political participation, often viewed as a tyranny of the majority. Thus our very individuality is being presented as incompatible with one participatory project in which sooner or later the former will be absorbed by the latter.

On the fear of politics

Hannah Arendt, a sagacious thinker who never neglected the importance of civil liberties, views this dilemma as strengthening representation at the expense of political participation. For her the essence of this logic is the superiority of the private and non-political over politics and democracy. Arendt views in this dilemma a shift in the meaning of freedom and warns us not to mistake this private logic with freedom nor "to equate these preliminaries of civilized government with the very substance of a free republic. For political freedom, generally speaking, means the right to be a participator in government or it means nothing."[120]

The anti-political essence of this heteronomous dilemma and the statist logic behind it is being masked in progressive terms as a fear for the minorities whose rights are threatened by one homogeneous whole. However, this view is steeped in parochial and romantic rhetoric invoking the need of an extra-social defender to protect the individual and the minority from the majoritarian monster. What they count on for protection are the institutions and mechanisms of negative freedom which the representative regime offers. Such institutions as constitutions restrict, prohibit, and suppress as does the bureaucratic repressive state apparatus.

The philosopher of autonomy Cornelius Castoriadis counters this logic with the suggestion that constitutional arrangements could also be contracted in one direct-democratic setting.[121] Why then should constitutional restraints fail in direct-democratic conditions and succeed in representative (oligarchic) ones? To this question we can only answer that there cannot be a constitution that will not be revised at some point in time, for even if it does not foresee it, it could then be changed by means of force if society deems it necessary. Castoriadis points toward the countless constitutions that have become just scraps of paper.[122] For constitutional arrangements can't stop people who are determined to bypass them. What one can do is act against the emergence of discriminative tendencies.

We can see today, as well as in many cases in history, that representativity is by no means the protector of individual and minoritarian liberties. Often politicians exploit xenophobic impulses that are latent in society to take hold of power. And as usual in representative democracy, those who elect them are also in the minority, because most often the majority consists of those who refuse to take part in the electoral process. Thus certain minorities manage to obtain some privileges but not political power because after the election day they can't participate in the political decision-making at the expense of the rest of the population. The German historian Robert Michels concludes that "the government, or the state, cannot be anything other than the organization of a minority. It is the aim of this minority to impose upon the rest of society a 'legal order' which is the outcome of the exigencies of dominion and of the exploitation of the mass..."[123]

For Castoriadis, the belief in the additional guarantee that representative (oligarchic) institutions contain for civil liberties is rooted in a tradition of certain historic reinterpretation of antiquity. This tradition tends to underline the negative moments in the historic experiences of direct democracy. And although Castoriadis himself does not negate the moments of folly of the Athenian demos, for example, he reminds us that "there have been elected, representative chambers that also have made bad decisions."[124] It is not the representatives that protect our liberties but certain arrangements that resulted not simply from the statesmen that have signed them, but by pressure exercised by large sections of society. And if they hold, it is because the populace is deeming it so, not some politician representatives.

For the advocates of the rights-or-participation dilemma, these arrangements and certain procedures that are designed to preserve them are not enough if they are not backed by the repressive apparatus of the state. According to Jacques Ranciere, this hatred of democracy is being expressed through the effort of the so-called rational state to tame the excessive popular passions.[125] Here again we see politics being sacrificed in the name of the private, because politics are only thinkable, as Ranciere suggests, when power is being allotted among all and not among the wisest, strongest, and most enlightened.[126]

Thus paradoxically the presupposed defenders of personal rights demand repression for the preservation of freedom. Punishment becomes the guardian of each individual, as long as he does not overstep certain boundaries, on whose determination however he does not have a say, thus diminishing his freedom and liberties. Here we should recall once again, the sobering logic of Hannah Arendt, who reminds us that "no punishment has ever possessed enough power of deterrence to prevent the commission of crimes. On the contrary, whatever the punishment, once a specific crime has appeared for the first time, its reappearance is more likely than its initial emergence could ever have been."[127]

Individuality and direct democracy

Contrary to what the defenders of statism and representativity would like us to believe, personal liberties and minoritarian rights are an integral part of direct democracy because its target is decentralizing power and thus the empowerment of every single individual. The theoretician of social ecology Murray Bookchin underlines the ways that debate, opposition, and dissent actually enrich the communal way of life and democratic processes.[128] Without them, he continues, society can turn into an "ideological cemetery" in which the hierarchical defenders of individualism stifle every dialectical idea, thus preventing the development of different individualities.

In the end, direct democracy is an inclusionary project that aims to create public space where various minorities and conscious individuals engage in dialectical and interrogative deliberation that results in the formation of an autonomous society. If one group decides to impose its opinion and disempower another one then, as Judith Butler explains, they are actually asking for a right to exclude, which is hardly democratic in intent or in effect.[129] Thus in this case we speak for an attempt at system change.

Direct-democratic responses to exclusion

Along with the more abstract arguments in favor of direct democracy, many have embarked on investigating, reshaping, and proposing more concrete mechanisms and institutions that potentially could tackle the attempts of certain social groups to hegemonize the democratic processes and exclude others from the decision-making. Such proposals range from sortition and rotation of key social and political positions so members of different minoritarian groups could hold them through mechanisms for constitutional upholding, to citizen juries for reviewing and vetoing popular decisions.

The Israeli advocate of direct democracy Aki Orr underlines the importance constitutions have in a direct-democratic setting. He suggests that while there should be the option of constitutional changes to be made by the popular decision-making bodies, such should be allowed only when a large majority is reached (he proposes 80 per cent of all the citizens).[130] Thus according to Orr an additional obstacle would be presented before large minorities with exclusionary intentions as well as before accidental or frivolous changes.

Castoriadis expands this logic and suggests that the administration of justice in a directly democratic society should be an additional task of already existing local decision-making institutions (in his vision he speaks of regional councils), functioning as lower courts in relation with putative offenses committed within their area of jurisdiction.[131] Although individual rights would be guaranteed by procedural rules established by the confederal decision-making bodies (which he calls central assemblies), citizens should have the right to appeal to their local council or assembly if they have felt any violation of their liberties.

Another approach to this problem comes from Stephen Shalom, author of the political participatory model ParPolity. In his vision of confederations of nested councils, the task of overseeing minoritarian and individual rights is delegated to council courts.[132] Shalom suggests that these courts should consist of 41 citizens chosen by lot that serve 2-year terms. For Shalom, this number allows simultaneously for a broad spectrum of social opinions to be represented while it remains small enough to allow for genuine deliberation to take place. The main purpose of these council courts should be to review decisions taken by deliberative decision-making bodies and veto them if they are in violation of human rights. Shalom's insistence on sortition over elections aims at overcoming the danger of exclusionary tendencies that are flourishing through populist electoralism.

Conclusion

We can conclude that the choice between participation and civil liberties is a pseudo-dilemma. There is no inherent contradiction between individual freedom and broad civic deliberation. Instead the one contributes for the development of the other. By its very nature direct democracy requires constant polemical debate and questioning of the "now," which demands the creation and maintenance of colorful and pluralist social amalgams. Mechanisms and institutions for the reproduction of this pluralism are already being investigated theoretically as well as having been tested in practice.

It is understandable that people can get anxious about their rights and freedoms when social change becomes a topic for consideration. The historic experiences of Nazism and its genocidal behavior toward minorities on the one hand, and tendencies for authoritarian socialism to trample on the individual rights of the Other have given enough reason for people to be wary when confronted with big promises for a brighter future. But we must not forget that in both of these cases there were extra-social statist mechanisms that didn't offer the expected protection while many people from below demonstrated maturity and often risked their own lives to help those less fortunate than themselves. Thus we can conclude that representativity and punishment are not guarantees for our freedom. Concrete measures backed by a conscious and politically active citizenry are far more likely to honor civil liberties. To achieve this goal there is the need for an active citizen culture created through popular involvement in political decision-making.

Endnotes

1. David Garrioch: "The Everyday Lives of Parisian Women and the 1789 French Revolution" in *Social History*, Vol. 24, No. 3 (Taylor & Francis, Ltd., 1999), pp. 231-249 (available online at https://www.jstor.org/stable/4286577).

2. https://www.resilience.org/stories/2017-06-07/history-future-solidarity-economy/

3. Eduardo Galeano: "Excerpts from the Works of Eduardo Galeano: Ventanas, Tejidos, Abrazos (Windows, Weavings, Embraces)" in *Fourth Genre: Explorations in Nonfiction*, vol. 3 no. 2 (2001): pp196-205.

4. Z Magazine (May 1998).

5. Cornelius Castoriadis: *The Rising Tide of Insignificancy: The Big Sleep* (unauthorized translation, 2003): pp350–351.

6. James Madison, Alexander Hamilton, and John Jay: *The Federalist Papers: The Classic Original Edition* (New York: SoHo Books, 2011): p26.

7. https://www.tandfonline.com/doi/abs/10.1558/crit.v12i3.396?journalCode=ycrh20

8. https://www.gisreportsonline.com/is-economic-inequality-a-bad-thing,politics,2459.html

9. https://www.theguardian.com/commentisfree/2015/dec/05/income-inequality-policy-capitalism

10. D. B. Krupp & Thomas R. Cook: "Local Competition Amplifies the Corrosive Effects of Inequality" in *SAGE Journals Volume: 29 issue: 5* (2018): pp824–833. (https://journals.sagepub.com/stoken/default+domain/10.1177/0956797617748419-free/full)

11. https://www.resilience.org/stories/2019-07-05/inequality-metrics-and-the-question-of-power/

12. http://peerproduction.net/issues/issue-1/invited-comments/a-new-communist-horizon/

13. www.salon.com/test3/2015/03/05/i_found_myself_
turning_into_an_idiot_david_graeber_explains_the_
life_sapping_reality_of_bureaucratic_life/?fbclid=I
wAR0SXKDal3xd4z2aqgYMV1FjxBzG8MyDpBXNy-
iChZZz43b0b8Sx1DBh2EM

14. http://reason.com/archives/1979/10/01/interview-with-
murray-bookchin/

15. Noam Chomsky: *Language and Politics* (California: AK
Press, 2004): p138.

16. https://libcom.org/library/municipalization-murray-
bookchin

17. https://libcom.org/library/municipalization-murray-
bookchin

18. https://libcom.org/library/municipalization-murray-
bookchin

19. Cornelius Castoriadis: *The Rising Tide of Insignificancy: The
Big Sleep* (unauthorized translation, 2003): p349.

20. Wolfgang Merkel and Sascha Kneip (eds.): *Democracy
and Crisis: Challenges in Turbulent Times* (Berlin: Springer
International Publishing, 2018): p253.

21. Dimitrios Roussopoulos: *The Rise of Cities* (Montreal: Black
Rose Books, 2017): p7.

22. https://qz.com/807733/in-the-future-cities-may-finally-
solve-problems-that-have-stumped-the-worlds-biggest-
nations/

23. https://www.forbes.com/sites/danielrunde/2015/02/24/
urbanization-development-opportunity/#42e7efaa6ca3

24. Antonio Negri: *Goodbye Mr Socialism* (New York: Seven
Stories Press 2006): p35.

25. https://globalparliamentofmayors.org/

26. https://www.compactofmayors.org/

27. https://www.icrc.org/en/international-review/war-in-
cities

28. https://www.forbes.com/sites/megacities/2011/04/04/the-

problem-with-megacities/#6dcd7a5b6f27

29. Antonio Negri: *Goodbye Mr Socialism* (New York: Seven Stories Press 2006): p35.

30. Simon Sadler: *The Situationist City* (Cambridge: The MIT Press, 1999): p157.

31. Richard Sennett: *The Fall of Public Man,* (New York: W. W. Norton & Company, 1992).

32. Richard Sennett: *The Fall of Public Man* (New York: W. W. Norton & Company, 1992), p261.

33. Peter G. Goheen: "Public space and the geography of the modern city" in *Progress in Human Geography* 22, Issue 4 (1998): p482.

34. https://www.dissentmagazine.org/online_articles/ neo-rurals-spain-lost-generation-economic-crash-rurbanization

35. *Journal of Urban Affairs*, Vol.36 No. I: p151.

36. Murray Bookchin: "Thoughts on Libertarian Municipalism" in *Left Green Perspectives*, Number 41, January 2000.

37. Murray Bookchin: *The Next Revolution* (New York: Verso, 2015): p34.

38. Murray Bookchin: *The Next Revolution* (New York: Verso, 2015): p73.

39. Murray Bookchin: *The Next Revolution* (New York: Verso, 2015): p35.

40. Charles Montgomery: *Happy City* (London: Penguin Books, 2015): p36.

41. https://journalistsresource.org/studies/environment/ cities/global-urban-expansion-impact-biodiversity-carbon-2030

42. https://www.commondreams.org/views/2015/10/23/good-place-everyone-walk

43. Donald Appleyard and Mark Lintell: "The Environmental Quality of Streets: The Resident's View Point" in *Journal of the American Planning Association,* (1972): pp84-101.

44. https://www.citylab.com/design/2014/10/why-12-foot-traffic-lanes-are-disastrous-for-safety-and-must-be-replaced-now/381117/

45. https://blog.nature.org/science/2015/05/22/science-nature-emotion-affect-feel-better/

46. Jane Jacobs: *The Death and Life of Great American Cities* (New York: Vintage Books, 1992): pp89-111.

47. Charles Montgomery: *Happy City*, (London: Penguin Books, 2013): p110.

48. Stuart Valins and Andrew Baum: *Residential Group Size, Social Interaction, and Crowding* in *Environment and Behavior* (1973)

49. David Harvey: "The right to the city" in *New Left Review, Vol.53* (September–October 2008).

50. David Harvey: *Rebel Cities* (New York: Verso Books, 2012): p117.

51. http://www.qmul.ac.uk/media/news/items/hss/178917.html

52. http://www.redpepper.org.uk/rebel-cities-the-citizen-platforms-in-power/

53. https://www.buzzfeed.com/jimdalrympleii/us-states-and-cities-react-to-paris-withdrawal?utm_term=.xmlReY3O3#.lgnX98G2G

54. http://new-compass.net/articles/olympia-all

55. TEV-DEM (or *Movement for Democratic Society*) is an alliance of local radical parties and social movements in northern Syria.

56. Where after the so called "Water Wars" (from December 1999 to April 2000) hundreds of water cooperatives were established by local communities that allowed them to directly manage the invaluable blue substance.

57. The citizens of Porto Alegre have determined their city's budget through a process of democratic deliberation and decision-making since 1989.

58. Rosemary Wakeman: *Practicing Utopia: An Intellectual History of the New Town Movement* (Chicago: The University of Chicago Press, 2016): p296.

59. Cornelius Castoriadis: *Figures of the Thinkable* (unauthorized translation, 2005): p146.

60. Ivan Illich: "Silence is a Commons" in *CoEvolution Quarterly* (1983).

61. Deirdre N. McCloskey. *The Bourgeois Virtues* (Chicago: The University of Chicago Press, 2006): p465.

62. Malthusianism originates from Thomas Malthus, a nineteenth-century clergyman, for whom the poor would always tend to use up their resources and remain in misery because of their fertility. (Derek Wall: *Economics After Capitalism* (London: Pluto Press, 2015): p125.)

63. The concept was based upon an essay written in 1833 by Lloyd, the Victorian economist, on the effects of unregulated grazing on common land and made widely-known by an article written by Hardin in 1968.

64. Theodoros Karyotis: "Chronicles of a Defeat Foretold" in *ROAR magazine*, Issue #0 (2015): pp32-63.

65. Michael Hardt & Antonio Negri: *Commonwealth* (Cambridge: The Belknap Press, 2011): pix.

66. David Bollier & Silke Helfrich: "Introduction: The Commons as a Transformative Vision" in *The Wealth of the Commons* (The Commons Strategy Group, 2012).

67. Ivan Illich: "Silence is a Commons" in *CoEvolution Quarterly* (1983).

68. Cornelius Castoriadis: "The Greek Polis and the Creation of Democracy" in *The Castoriadis Reader* (Oxford: Blackwell, 1997): p280.

69. http://bollier.org/blog/anthropologist-harry-walker-lessons-amazonian-commons

70. http://www.onthecommons.org/magazine/elinor-ostroms-8-principles-managing-commmons

71. Elinor Ostrom in Nobel Prize lecture *Beyond Markets and States: Polycentric Governance of Complex Economic Systems* (2009).
72. http://whatis.techtarget.com/definition/digital-commons
73. Cornelius Castoriadis: *Democracy and Relativism* (unauthorized translation, 2013): p41.
74. Cengiz Gunes and Welat Zeydanlioglu: *The Kurdish Question in Turkey* (London: Routledge, 2014): p191.
75. For example Ostrom in *Beyond Markets and States: Polycentric Governance of Complex Economic Systems* (2009) and Harvey in *Rebel Cities*, 2012. p.69
76. Especially after the financial crisis of 2008.
77. http://siteresources.worldbank.org/INTWSS/Resources/WN5cooperatives.pdf
78. http://peerproduction.net/issues/issue-7-policies-for-the-commons/peer-reviewed-papers/towards-a-new-reconfiguration-among-the-state-civil-society-and-the-market/
79. Hannah Arendt: *The Human Condition* (Chicago: The University of Chicago, 1998): p53.
80. http://www.versobooks.com/blogs/1612-thought-is-the-courage-of-hopelessness-an-interview-with-philosopher-giorgio-agamben
81. http://www.footprintnetwork.org/en/index.php/GFN/page/public_data_package
82. http://www.intress.info/fileadmin/intress-docs/Perspectives_and_assumptions_for_setting_resource_targets_01.pdf
83. http://www.nature.com/news/environment-waste-production-must-peak-this-century-1.14032
84. https://theconversation.com/earths-sixth-mass-extinction-has-begun-new-study-confirms-43432
85. https://en.wikipedia.org/wiki/Great_Pacific_garbage_patch

86. http://ec.europa.eu/clima/policies/international/negotiations/paris/index_en.htm

87. http://www.aljazeera.com/indepth/opinion/2013/04/201349124135226392.html

88. Errico Malatesta: *At the Cafe: Conversations on Anarchism* (London: Freedom Press, 2005): p30.

89. http://greece.greekreporter.com/2016/08/23/cabinet-discusses-fair-growth-and-governments-work-ahead-of-tif/

90. Naomi Klein: *This Changes Everything* (London: Penguin Books, 2015): pp180-182.

91. https://roarmag.org/magazine/socialize-the-internet/

92. Elinor Ostrom: *Beyond Markets and States: Polycentric Governance of Complex Economic Systems*, Nobel-Prize Lecture (2009).

93. David Graeber: *The Utopia of Rules* (London: Melville House, 2015): p110.

94. The N. Dakota project was reinstated by Trump in 2017 and is now operating as an oil pipeline, despite legal victories confirming its illegitimacy.

95. https://nacla.org/article/new-water-wars-bolivia-climate-change-and-indigenous-struggle

96. http://www.aljazeera.com/indepth/opinion/2011/06/201162995115833636.html

97. *Solidarity Economies: A Guerrilla War Against Capitalism* (available online on: http://www.huffingtonpost.com/beverly-bell/solidarity-economies-a-gu_b_5479762.html).

98. Pierre Clastres: *Society Against the State: Essays in Political Anthropology* (New York: Zone Books, 1989).

99. See Peter Kropotkin: *Mutual Aid: A Factor of Evolution* (Montreal: Black Rose Books, 1989).

100. Ethan Miller: "Other Economies Are Possible!" in *Building a Solidarity Economy* (available online on: http://www.geo.coop/node/35).

101. Roberto Frenkel: "Globalization and financial crisis in Latin America" in *CEPAL Review*, No.80 (2003).
102. https://en.wikipedia.org/wiki/Solidarity_economy #Social_and_solidarity_economy
103. http://www.geo.coop/archives/SolidarityEcono micsEthanMiller.htm
104. Karl Polanyi: *The Fascist Virus*, 18-8, n.d.
105. Cornelius Castoriadis: *The Problem of Democracy Today* (available online on: http://www.athene.antenna.nl/ ARCHIEF/NR01-Athene/02-Probl.-e.html).
106. Cornelius Castoriadis: "Sur le Contenu du Socialisme" in *Socialisme ou Barbarie*, issue 22 (1957).
107. http://www.co-intelligence.org/CIPol_democSoc PwrAnal.html
108. Hannah Arendt: *The Origins of Totalitarianism* (London: Houghton Mifflin Harcourt, 1973): p353.
109. https://www.researchgate.net/publication/311097154_ Why_Education_Predicts_Decreased_Belief_in_ Conspiracy_Theories_Education_and_Conspiracy_Beliefs
110. https://www.csmonitor.com/Commentary/2020/0731/ Tracking-the-anti-science-wave-Commentary-on-the-roots-of-distrust https://pdfs.semanticscholar.org/fb37/6e c072778e717591b8424187230d39b86724.pdf
111. https://www.psychologicalscience.org/news/conspiracy-beliefs-linked-with-search-for-certainty-security-and-social-desires.html
112. http://new-compass.net/articles/bookchin-%C3%B6calan-and-dialectics-democracy
113. https://journals.sagepub.com/doi/10.1177/09637 21417718261
114. https://journals.sagepub.com/doi/10.1177/0963 721417718261
115. https://www.psychologicalscience.org/news/conspiracy-beliefs-linked-with-search-for-certainty-security-and-

social-desires.html

116. http://www.hartford-hwp.com/archives/10/125.html

117. https://pdfs.semanticscholar.org/fb37/6ec072778e717591b 8424187230d39b86724.pdf

118. Joseph E. Uscinski: *Conspiracy Theories and the People Who Believe Them* (Oxford: Oxford University Press, 2018): p433.

119. Cornelius Castoriadis: *Democracy and Relativism* (unauthorized translation, 2013): p49.

120. Hannah Arendt: *On Revolution* (London: Penguin Classics, 2006): p210.

121. Cornelius Castoriadis: *Democracy and Relativism* (unauthorized translation, 2013): p50.

122. Cornelius Castoriadis: *Democracy and Relativism* (unauthorized translation, 2013): p50.

123. Robert Michels: *Political Parties: A Sociological Study of the Oligarchical Tendencies of Modern Democracy* (New York: Heart's International Library Company, 1915): p390.

124. Cornelius Castoriadis: *Democracy and Relativism* (unauthorized translation, 2013): p51.

125. Jacques Ranciere: *Hatred of Democracy* (New York: Verso Books 2015): p8.

126. Jacques Ranciere: *Democracy in What State* (New York: Columbia University Press, 2012): pp78-79.

127. Hannah Arendt: "Epilogue" in *Eichmann in Jerusalem* (New York: Viking Press 1963).

128. Murray Bookchin: "Communalism: The Democratic Dimension of Anarchism" in *Democracy and Nature*, vol. 8: p9.

129. http://www.zeit.de/kultur/2016-10/judith-butler-donald-trump-populism-interview

130. Aki Orr: *Politics Without Politicians* (self-published, 2005): p22.

131. Cornelius Castoriadis: *Workers' Councils and the Economy*

of the Self-Managed Society (Johannesburg: Zabalaza Books, 2007): p69.

132. https://zcomm.org/znetarticle/parpolity-political-vision-for-a-good-society-by-stephen1-shalom/

Bibliography

Biehl, Janet. *The Politics of Social Ecology: Libertarian Municipalism.* Montreal: Black Rose Books, 1997.

Bollier, David & Helfrich, Silke. *The Wealth of the Commons: A World Beyond Market and State.* Massachusetts: Levellers Press, 2015.

Bookchin, Murray. *The Next Revolution: Popular Assemblies and the Promise of Direct Democracy.* New York: Verso, 2015.

Bookchin, Murray. *The Philosophy of Social Ecology: Essays on Dialectical Naturalism,* Montreal: Black Rose Books, 1996.

Bookchin, Murray. *Urbanization without Cities: The Rise and Decline of Citizenship.* Montreal: Black Rose Books, 1996.

Butler, Judith. *Notes Toward a Performative Theory of Assembly.* Cambridge: Harvard University Press, 2015.

Cabannes, Yves & Delgado, Cecilia. *Another City is possible with Participatory Budgeting.* Montreal: Black Rose Books, 2017.

Campbell, Debra & Crittenden, Jack. *Direct Deliberative Democracy: How Citizens Can Rule.* Montreal: Black Rose Books, 2019.

Cardan, Paul (Castoriadis). *History and Revolution: a revolutionary critique of historical materialism.* Solidarity Pamphlet No38, 1971.

Castoriadis, Cornelius. *A Society Adrift.* unauthorized translation, 2010. (Available online at http://www.notbored.org/ASA.pdf)

Castoriadis, Cornelius. *Democracy and Relativism: Discussion with the "MAUSS" Group.* unauthorized translation, 2013. (Available online at http://www.notbored.org/DR.pdf)

Castoriadis, Cornelius. *Figures of the Thinkable (including "Passion and Knowledge").* unauthorized translation, 2005. (Available online at http://www.notbored.org/FTPK.pdf)

Castoriadis, Cornelius. *History as Creation.* London: Solidarity

Pamphlet, No.54, 1978.

Castoriadis, Cornelius. *Postscript on Insignificancy.* unauthorized translation, 2017. (Available online at http://www.notbored. org/PSRTI.pdf)

Castoriadis, Cornelius. *Political and Social Writings Volume 1.* Minneapolis: University of Minnesota Press, 1988.

Castoriadis, Cornelius. *Political and Social Writings Volume 2.* Minneapolis: University of Minnesota Press, 1988.

Castoriadis, Cornelius. *Political and Social Writings Volume 3.* Minneapolis: University of Minnesota Press, 1993.

Castoriadis, Cornelius. *The Imaginary Institution of Society.* Cambridge: The MIT Press, 1998.

Castoriadis, Cornelius. *The Rising Tide of Insignificancy: The Big Sleep.* unauthorized translation, 2003. (Available online at http://www.notbored.org/RTI.pdf)

Castoriadis, Cornelius. *Workers' Councils and the Economics of a Self-Managed Society.* Johannesburg: Zabalaza Books, 2007.

Curtis, David Ames (Editor). *The Castoriadis Reader.* Oxford: Blackwell Publishers, 1997.

Davis, Mike. *Planet of Slums.* New York: Verso, 2007.

Graham, Stephen. *Cities under Siege: The new Military Urbanism.* New York: Verso, 2011.

Harvey, David. *Rebel Cities: From the Right to the City to the Urban Revolution.* New York: Verso, 2012.

Jacobs, Jane. *The Death and Life of Great American Cities.* New York: Vintage Books, 1992.

Knapp, Ayboga & Flach. *Revolution in Rojava: Democratic Autonomy and Women's Liberation in the Syrian Kurdistan.* London: Pluto Press, 2016.

Lefebvre, Henri. *Rhythmanalysis: Space, Time and Everyday Life.* London: Bloomsbury, 2013.

Lefebvre, Henri. *The Production of Space.* Oxford: Blackwell, 1991.

Montgomery, Charles. *Happy City.* London: Penguin Books,

2015.

Negri, Antonio. *Goodbye Mr Socialism.* New York: Seven Stories Press, 2006.

Negri, Antonio & Hardt, Michael. *Commonwealth.* Cambridge: The Belknap Press, 2011.

Ocalan, Abdullah. *Democratic Confederalism.* Cologne: International Initiative, 2011.

Ocalan, Abdullah. *Liberating Life: Woman's Revolution.* Cologne: International Initiative, 2013.

Ostrom, Elinor. *Governing the Commons: The Evolution of Institutions for Collective Action.* Cambridge: Cambridge University Press, 2015.

Ross, Kristin. *The Emergence of Social Space.* New York: Verso, 2008.

Roussopoulos, Dimitrios. *The Rise of Cities.* Montreal: Black Rose Books, 2017.

Roussopoulos, Dimitrios. *Participatory Democracy: Prospects for Democratizing Democracy.* Montreal: Black Rose Books, 2003.

Roussopoulos, Dimitrios. *Political Ecology: Beyond Environmentalism.* Porsgrunn: New Compass Press, 2015.

Sadler, Simon. *The Situationist City.* Cambridge: The MIT Press, 1999.

Sennett, Richard. *The Fall of Public Man.* New York: W. W. Norton & Company, 1992.

Wakeman, Rosemary. *Practicing Utopia: An Intellectual History of the New Town Movement.* Chicago: The University of Chicago Press, 2016.

Wright, Erik Olin. *Envisioning Real Utopias.* New York: Verso, 2010.

Wright, Erik Olin & Fung, Archon. *Deepening Democracy: Institutional Innovations in Empowered Participatory Governance.* New York: Verso, 2003.

Afterword

By Mark Mason

Yavor Tarinski tears apart the TINA claim that there is no alternative to capitalist living. We are the many. They are the few. The manner in which the few exploit the many is through a combination of state repressive police violence and corporate-state schooling and mass-media propaganda and obedience training.

The status of class consciousness today in the USA is significantly retrograde. Labor union membership is about one-fourth of what it was in 1920, and corporations possess much more economic and political power. The class war is being lost as the corporate-state charges off in the direction of infinite growth by means of infinite plunder of all forms of Earth and life. As capitalism commands ecosystem collapse, Mr Tarinski's summation of our existential challenge exhibits a clarity necessary for creative, life-affirming rearrangements of power. Politics is the art of deception. The solidarity economy evaporates politics and politicians, replacing the dual parent-child dyad of the citizen-state and the worker-boss. Belonging emerges from servitude. The mask of silent pseudo-civilcs reveals itself as the mask of the false persona of patriarchy, patriotism, colonial white supremacy, objectification of the biosphere, and the acquired mantel of psychic death. Solidarity or extinction.

The dominant death-instinct culture dwells in denials. Oblivious, school teachers do not teach and journalists do not inform. Priests and politicians alike stultify social discourse. Celebrities of the statehouse exhibit atavistic slogans of stillborn liberal reforms. The system not only cannot fix itself, it cannot bring itself to convene a truth-and-reconciliation commission.

Capitalism the death cult. All political and economic agency now resides behind the corporate doors of pathological pursuits of private profit.

Never has the vital vocabulary of socioeconomic integration and participation been more important. Mr Tarinksi has delivered us from forms of corporate cognitive conscription. Now, superfluous labels fall away. Let us take up appropriate direct action in the historical context of liberation struggles. Authenticity and autonomy arise. The common good and the commons return from deep psychic repression. Rebirth of the Self. Transformation. The Potemkin village is abandoned. Possibilities.

Biographies

Yavor Tarinski is an independent researcher and militant in social movements. He is currently a member of the editorial board of the Greek libertarian journal aftoleksi.gr, part of the administrative board of the Transnational Institute of Social Ecology, as well as bibliographer at Agora International. Author of the books *Direct Democracy: Context, Society, Individuality* (Cork: Durty Books, 2019), *Short Introduction to the Political Legacy of Castoriadis* (Athens: Aftoleksi, 2020), and *Common Futures: Social Transformation and Political Ecology* (Montreal: Black Rose Books, 2020)

Emet Değirmenci was a co-founder of the *Social Ecology* group in Turkey in the 90s (http://ekoloji.org/). She is an independent researcher and has published the book *Kadinlar Ecolojik Donusumde* [*Women's Activism in Ecological Transformation*] (Yeni İnsan Yayınevi, 2010), as well as being co-editor of the anthology *Social Ecology and the Right to the City* (TRISE, 2019). Her writings have appeared in a variety of magazines such as Permaculture Activist in the US and Social Ecology Magazine in Turkey.

Dr Mark Mason was trained as a biological anthropologist educated at the University of California, Berkeley, and was engaged in the Occupy and bioregional green and peace social movements. He offers analyses of United States' domestic and foreign policies for the international news media.

CULTURE, SOCIETY & POLITICS

Contemporary culture has eliminated the concept and public figure of the intellectual. A cretinous anti-intellectualism presides, cheer-led by hacks in the pay of multinational corporations who reassure their bored readers that there is no need to rouse themselves from their stupor. Zer0 Books knows that another kind of discourse - intellectual without being academic, popular without being populist - is not only possible: it is already flourishing. Zer0 is convinced that in the unthinking, blandly consensual culture in which we live, critical and engaged theoretical reflection is more important than ever before.

If you have enjoyed this book, why not tell other readers by posting a review on your preferred book site.

You may also wish to
subscribe to our Zer0 Books YouTube Channel.

Bestsellers from Zer0 Books include:

Give Them An Argument
Logic for the Left
Ben Burgis
Many serious leftists have learned to distrust talk of logic. This
is a serious mistake.
Paperback: 978-1-78904-210-8 ebook: 978-1-78904-211-5

Poor but Sexy
Culture Clashes in Europe East and West
Agata Pyzik
How the East stayed East and the West stayed West.
Paperback: 978-1-78099-394-2 ebook: 978-1-78099-395-9

An Anthropology of Nothing in Particular
Martin Demant Frederiksen
A journey into the social lives of meaninglessness.
Paperback: 978-1-78535-699-5 ebook: 978-1-78535-700-8

In the Dust of This Planet
Horror of Philosophy vol. 1 Eugene Thacker
In the first of a series of three books on the Horror of
Philosophy, *In the Dust of This Planet* offers the genre of horror
as a way of thinking about the unthinkable.
Paperback: 978-1-84694-676-9 ebook: 978-1-78099-010-1

The End of Oulipo?
An Attempt to Exhaust a Movement
Lauren Elkin, Veronica Esposito
Paperback: 978-1-78099-655-4 ebook: 978-1-78099-656-1

Capitalist Realism
Is There No Alternative?
Mark Fisher
An analysis of the ways in which capitalism has presented
itself as the only realistic political-economic system.
Paperback: 978-1-84694-317-1 ebook: 978-1-78099-734-6

Rebel Rebel
Chris O'Leary
David Bowie: every single song. Everything you want to know,
everything you didn't know.
Paperback: 978-1-78099-244-0 ebook: 978-1-78099-713-1

Kill All Normies
Angela Nagle
Online culture wars from 4chan and Tumblr to Trump.
Paperback: 978-1-78535-543-1 ebook: 978-1-78535-544-8

Cartographies of the Absolute
Alberto Toscano, Jeff Kinkle
An aesthetics of the economy for the twenty-first century.
Paperback: 978-1-78099-275-4 ebook: 978-1-78279-973-3

Malign Velocities
Accelerationism and Capitalism
Benjamin Noys
Long listed for the Bread and Roses Prize 2015, *Malign
Velocities* argues against the need for speed, tracking
acceleration as the symptom of the ongoing crises of
capitalism.
Paperback: 978-1-78279-300-7 ebook: 978-1-78279-299-4

Meat Market
Female Flesh under Capitalism
Laurie Penny
A feminist dissection of women's bodies as the fleshy fulcrum
of capitalist cannibalism, whereby women are both consumers
and consumed.
Paperback: 978-1-84694-521-2 ebook: 978-1-84694-782-7

Babbling Corpse
Vaporwave and the Commodification of Ghosts
Grafton Tanner
Paperback: 978-1-78279-759-3 ebook: 978-1-78279-760-9

New Work New Culture
Work we want and a culture that strengthens us
Frithjof Bergmann
A serious alternative for mankind and the planet.
Paperback: 978-1-78904-064-7 ebook: 978-1-78904-065-4

Romeo and Juliet in Palestine
Teaching Under Occupation
Tom Sperlinger
Life in the West Bank, the nature of pedagogy and the role of a
university under occupation.
Paperback: 978-1-78279-637-4 ebook: 978-1-78279-636-7

Color, Facture, Art and Design
Iona Singh
This materialist definition of fine-art develops guidelines for
architecture, design, cultural-studies and ultimately social
change.
Paperback: 978-1-78099-629-5 ebook: 978-1-78099-630-1

Sweetening the Pill
or How We Got Hooked on Hormonal Birth Control Holly
Grigg-Spall
Has contraception liberated or oppressed women?
Sweetening the Pill breaks the silence on the dark side of
hormonal contraception.
Paperback: 978-1-78099-607-3 ebook: 978-1-78099-608-0

Why Are We The Good Guys?
Reclaiming Your Mind from the Delusions of Propaganda
David Cromwell
A provocative challenge to the standard ideology that Western
power is a benevolent force in the world.
Paperback: 978-1-78099-365-2 ebook: 978-1-78099-366-9

The Writing on the Wall
On the Decomposition of Capitalism and its Critics Anselm
Jappe, Alastair Hemmens
A new approach to the meaning of social emancipation.
Paperback: 978-1-78535-581-3 ebook: 978-1-78535-582-0

Enjoying It
Candy Crush and Capitalism
Alfie Bown
A study of enjoyment and of the enjoyment of studying. Bown
asks what enjoyment says about us and what we say about
enjoyment, and why.
Paperback: 978-1-78535-155-6 ebook: 978-1-78535-156-3

Ghosts of My Life
Writings on Depression, Hauntology and Lost Futures
Mark Fisher
Paperback: 978-1-78099-226-6 ebook: 978-1-78279-624-4

Neglected or Misunderstood
The Radical Feminism of Shulamith Firestone
Victoria Margree
An interrogation of issues surrounding gender, biology,
sexuality, work and technology, and the ways in which our
imaginations continue to be in thrall to ideologies of maternity
and the nuclear family.
Paperback: 978-1-78535-539-4 ebook: 978-1-78535-540-0

How to Dismantle the NHS in 10 Easy Steps (Second Edition)
Youssef El-Gingihy
The story of how your NHS was sold off and why you will
have to buy private health insurance soon. A new expanded
second edition with chapters on junior doctors' strikes and
government blueprints for US-style healthcare.
Paperback: 978-1-78904-178-1 ebook: 978-1-78904-179-8

Digesting Recipes
The Art of Culinary Notation
Susannah Worth
A recipe is an instruction, the imperative tone of the expert,
but this constraint can offer its own kind of potential. A recipe
need not be a domestic trap but might instead offer escape –
something to fantasise about or aspire to.
Paperback: 978-1-78279-860-6 ebook: 978-1-78279-859-0

Most titles are published in paperback and as an ebook.
Paperbacks are available in traditional bookshops. Both print
and ebook formats are available online.
Follow us at:
https://www.facebook.com/ZeroBooks
https://twitter.com/Zer0Books
https://www.instagram.com/zero.Books